NO FLUMMERY

recipes from
MICHAEL LEAR

authorHOUSE®

AuthorHouse™ UK Ltd.
500 Avebury Boulevard
Central Milton Keynes, MK9 2BE
www.authorhouse.co.uk
Phone: 08001974150

First published by AuthorHouse 11/22/2011

ISBN: 978-1-4567-7313-7 (sc)

Any people depicted in stock imagery provided by Thinkstock are models,
and such images are being used for illustrative purposes only.
Certain stock imagery © Thinkstock.

This book is printed on acid-free paper.

Because of the dynamic nature of the Internet, any web addresses or links contained in this book may have changed
since publication and may no longer be valid. The views expressed in this work are solely those of the author and do
not necessarily reflect the views of the publisher, and the publisher hereby disclaims any responsibility for them.

Back cover photograph: courtesy of Barbara Bristow.
Proofreading: my grateful thanks to Angela Portman.

This book is dedicated to Angela

CONTENTS

INTRODUCTION

Oh Lord – I hear you say - not another cookery book!

I will emphasise straightaway that this is not a Cookery Book; it is a Recipe Book. Whilst one certainly does not need to be a 'cordon bleu' or highly experienced cook to handle these recipes, I have assumed a reasonable basic knowledge of practical cooking techniques and, more importantly, a genuine wish to produce interesting and appetising meals – whether for a family, a supper for two, a dinner party or a casual occasion with friends. The recipes are not original, although many of my variations may be, but are quite simply the accumulated sum of my own modest cooking experience.

The word 'Flummery' is defined in the OED as "empty compliments, trifles, nonsense" but I prefer the definition in the Penguin Dictionary of "pretentious humbug or hypocritical deception or pretence". It can, of course, also mean a sweet dish from Wales usually made with flour or oatmeal, eggs, honey and cream. You won't find the latter and I hope not the former in this book.

My mother was, and still is, an excellent, practical and imaginative cook and so I have always enjoyed good food, but it wasn't until my early 20's that I was inspired to try for myself by my friend Ian, with his neatly sewn up stuffed trout, and who had a wonderful repertoire from the 'Penguin Cookery Book for Beginners', when we were house sharing. Soon after that many enjoyable trips to France opened ones eyes to the wonders of Gallic cuisine and other such possibilities.

I am still amazed by how very few men cook in a domestic situation, given that most top chefs are men, and yet cooking is the most wonderfully therapeutic occupation; just enough concentration required to keep one's mind from the worries of the world, but an immediately satisfying and practical pastime/hobby/interest. When your biggest worry is whether a sauce will curdle, if the fish is overcooked or whether a meal will be ready on time then you may not know it, but you have cracked one of life's big secrets!

Why did I decide to write this book? I am a Jack of All Trades and master of none. I wanted to record for easy reference all my own favourite recipes; after doing a computer course I was tempted to construct a recipe database; I feel strongly that too many commercial cookery and recipe books are not written in the easiest to follow of consumer formats; it is a personal indulgence; it has been quite a challenge, but fun; I enjoy cooking and communicating.

PRACTICAL MATTERS – most of my cooking has been in a 4 oven Aga and I suspect many of my likely readers will be Aga users. Really very serious cooks will use gas, but the obvious traditional aspects of an Aga are hard to beat. Most recipes are for 4-5 people, but appetites vary and one should use one's own judgement. Quantities seldom need to be too precise, but it would be silly to put 'about' before every measure. Reluctantly I decided to use metric measurements, although I suppose I could have done both; rather fussy. Although most of my generation will tend to think imperial I would like my book to be 'in print' for years to come!

I cannot over emphasise the importance of READING THROUGH A RECIPE very carefully before starting. Success involves total commitment. When the phone rings halfway through, ignore it! Apart from the simplest of recipes it is most important to have a very clear idea of what you are going to do, and how you will achieve it, before you start.

NOTES – I am a great believer in jotting down observations in cookery books and for that reason each recipe has a small space for 'notes'; that is why this book is printed on matt, not glossy paper; so that the ink doesn't run! It is not intended as a coffee table decoration.

A word on GARLIC, which figures in so many recipes; the raw pungency comes from the cut surface being exposed; so the more finely cut the stronger it will be. When crushed and chopped the flavour will be most intense, less so when coarsely chopped, less so when sliced and when left whole - there is the well known chicken recipe using 40 whole garlic cloves where the end result is simply a mild and delicate but delicious aroma – as in garlic soup. When fried hot and alone garlic becomes quite bitter, so add it after other ingredients, such as onions or whatever; although in some Indian dishes this bitterness can be used as a garnish. The longer cooked the more it loses intensity; so add it sooner or later depending on the desired effect. An easy way to peel a garlic clove is to give it a gentle bash with a mallet or your fist, when it will just slip out. No need for a garlic press, hell to clean. Finally, whole unskinned garlic cloves when baked can be squeezed out and the resulting delicately delicious mush can enhance many different dishes.

SEASONING, HERBS AND SPICES – always use freshly ground black pepper and sea salt if possible. Keep a good store of whole spices to hand and grind them when needed using a small coffee grinder. Wonderful aromas! Herbs are easily grown and a well stocked herb garden close to the kitchen door is an absolute godsend. Bought in little jars from supermarkets etc they are incredibly expensive. We had a bay tree at North Aston which I reckoned at Tesco retail prices was worth well over £10,000!

PRESENTATION - although quality of ingredients is of prime importance I do think that with any dish the single most important factor is in its appearance; and this can so easily be achieved. A scattering of a few chopped herbs, a swirl of cream or crème fraîche, a few croutons in a soup, careful arrangement of ingredients on the plate or serving dish, all help to enhance the pleasure and anticipation of a good meal. Useful garnishes, where appropriate, could also be fried parsley, chopped egg whites or yolks, diced tomato or cucumber flesh, olives, anchovies, chives in particular or their lovely mauve flowers.

The INDEX, apart from listing the recipes, also lists the ingredients. So if you have a surplus of something you can look it up and find a recipe to use it in.

This book is divided into sections of my own choosing, but the boundaries between them can be very grey, and of course it does not really matter at all. Flexibility and imaginative variation are all important; as is the ability to use whatever ingredients are available. HAVE FUN.

Michael Lear
Bledington
10th November 2010

SOUP

Basil and tomato soup
Broccoli and stilton soup
Butternut squash and apple soup
Chilled cucumber soup
Cucumber vichyssoise
French onion soup
Gazpacho Andaluz
Leek and chickpea soup
Portuguese cabbage soup
Potage bonne femme
Russian cucumber and spinach soup
Vichyssoise

I F SOUP HAS traditionally been one of the mainstays of good French home cooking, then stock is undoubtedly at the heart of most good soups. Stock cubes are an excellent substitute; although with carefully chosen ingredients using just water can still give superbly tasty soups.

A stock is so easily made. In 3-4 pints of water, simmer for a couple of hours anything from a chicken carcase, beef, lamb or fish bones, together with half a chopped onion, a bit of carrot or celery, say, and lots of seasoning. Strain, cool and skim off the fat, and there it is – perfect home made stock which will keep for several days in the fridge or can be frozen.

Here I have included a range of my own favourite soups. Some to warm in winter, some to enliven the taste buds, chilled summer soups, some that just look good and others which use up whatever is leftover in the kitchen. Practically anything can be made into a soup and experimentation is always fun.

After many family meals some vegetables will remain. Liquidise these, perhaps adding some chopped onion or garlic. Stir in stock and you may be amazed by the result.

Most soups are made with vegetable or salad ingredients and an important tip to get right with most of them is the initial sweating in butter which adds so much richness to the taste, whether stock is used or not.

Presentation is so important with any recipe and, with soup, this would include serving from an attractive tureen with a proper soup ladle, a scattering of chopped herbs, a swirl of cream or *crème fraîche*, or perhaps *croûtons* to decorate. Chopped chives are always good as they add a tasty little tang to most dishes.

1

BASIL AND TOMATO SOUP

A fresh tasting chilled summer soup that can be put together in a few minutes

2 x 14oz tins chopped tomatoes
lime (or lemon) juice
1-2 cloves garlic
seasoning and sugar
handful of basil leaves
chives
125ml crème fraîche
cucumber slices

NOTES

Crush the garlic, shred the basil and chop the chives.

Put the tomatoes into a food processor with a generous squeeze of lime juice, the garlic, seasoning and sugar to taste, and the basil.

Blend well and add the *crème fraîche* and blend again to a smooth *purée*. Put into a serving bowl.

Chill well and float very thin slices of cucumber on top. Sprinkle with chopped chives.

TIPS AND VARIATIONS-

- use fresh tomatoes if very ripe and skinned
- a little water can be added to get the right consistency
- if you put the tinned tomatoes in the fridge first it barely needs chilling
- use yoghurt in place of *crème fraîche* for a lighter consistency

BROCCOLI AND STILTON SOUP

*One way of using up some of that overambitious Christmas stilton
when you tire of eating it or it starts to dry out*

1 large head of broccoli

1 medium onion

3 medium potatoes

butter

250g stilton cheese

500ml stock

seasoning

NOTES

Coarsely chop the onion. Cut the florets from the broccoli and chop all the tender parts of the stem. Peel and roughly chop the potatoes. Crumble the stilton.

Gently fry the onion and potato for a few minutes in some butter until softening. Add the broccoli and stir around until the butter is absorbed. Season to taste.

Add most of the stock and simmer for 15-20 minutes when the vegetables should be cooked through. Let it cool a little and stir in the stilton.

Liquidise in the blender but leaving a little texture to the soup. Add more stock to get your preferred consistency. Serve with a few pieces of crumbled stilton on top.

TIPS AND VARIATIONS-

- add a clove or two of crushed garlic when frying the onion
- add some cream to make it smoother
- use Irish Casheel instead of Stilton – or any other left over blue cheese
- reheats very well

BUTTERNUT SQUASH AND APPLE SOUP

Quick and easy to make and a really delicious combination of flavours

1tbs sunflower oil

1 medium onion

2tsps curry powder

2 eating apples

1 medium butternut squash

seasoning

1 litre light stock

NOTES

Chop the onion. Peel the squash and chop into small pieces. Peel, core and slice the apple.

Soften the onion in the oil in a large pan for a few minutes without browning. Add the curry powder and stir in well. Add the squash and the apple, and stir around for a few minutes to absorb the oil.

Add the stock and simmer for 20-30 minutes. Check seasoning, liquidise and serve.

TIPS AND VARIATIONS-

- add more stock if too thick
- any good curry paste will do just as well
- press through a sieve for smoother finish
- whilst a properly made stock is best, stock cubes or even just water will do well
- decorate with a swirl of cream or yoghourt, and chopped parsley
- very good hot or cold and improves with 24 hours in the fridge
- you could add a little chopped ginger and garlic to spice it up a bit

CHILLED CUCUMBER SOUP
A light and refreshing salad soup for a warm summer's day

2 cucumbers
juice of a lemon
500ml vegetable stock
200ml double cream, chilled
handful of chives and parsley
seasoning

NOTES

Save 6-8 thin slices of cucumber for later decoration. Roughly chop the cucumbers, unpeeled; finely chop the chives and the parsley.

Cover the cucumber pieces with the lemon juice, stock, chives, parsley and seasonings. Chill for an hour or two and, at the same time, chill the cream.

Put everything, except the cream, into a blender and liquidise until it becomes a creamy green *purée*. Add the chilled cream, adjust seasoning to taste and blend again.

Serve in individual bowls each decorated with a cucumber slice and an ice cube or two.

TIPS AND VARIATIONS-
- peel, or part peel, and deseed the cucumbers if you prefer
- take care to get the seasoning right or it may be a bit bland
- use a stock cube if you wish
- yoghurt or *crème fraîche* can be a lighter substitute for the cream
- try adding chopped gherkins, garlic, spring onions or mint
- vary the proportions to get the consistency you prefer – cucumbers are very watery and you may need less stock

CUCUMBER VICHYSSOISE

Another good use for surplus cucumbers – serve hot or cold – but cold is best

500g new potatoes   NOTES
1 cucumber
125g butter
1 medium onion
1 litre chicken stock
1 tsp sugar
seasoning
125ml cream

Cut the potatoes and unpeeled cucumber into chunky pieces and chop the onion.

Melt the butter in a large pan on a gentle heat. Stir in the vegetables, cover and simmer for 10 minutes or so, stirring occasionally, until slightly softened and the butter absorbed.

Add the stock, bring back to the boil, and simmer, covered, for another 15-20 minutes, or until the vegetables are just tender.

Blend in a food processor until smooth – push through a sieve if you are very keen! Let it cool a little, then stir in the sugar, seasoning and cream. Serve hot or chilled as is your mood.

TIPS AND VARIATIONS-

* peel the cucumbers if you prefer
* stir frequently with a wooden spoon at all stages
* decorate with chopped parsley
* a hand held processor enables you to leave in a few chunks of cucumber and potato which adds a 'rustic' texture
* use more or less stock to get your preferred consistency

FRENCH ONION SOUP

A quickly made winter warmer and a guaranteed cure for colds

2-3 large Spanish onions
1 tbs olive oil
50g butter
2-3 tsps sugar
1 litre beef stock
seasoning

grated gruyère or parmesan
bread croûtes

NOTES

Slice the onions very thinly, cover, and cook very gently in the oil and butter in a large heavy pan until soft, about 20-30 minutes.

Sprinkle over the sugar, increase the heat a little and stir, uncovered, for several minutes until the sugar lightly caramelises.

Add the stock and seasoning, stir, cover, and simmer gently for 20-30 minutes.

Meanwhile make the *croûtes* by baking slices of french bread in a slow oven for 30 minutes until lightly browned.

Put the *croûtes* in a tureen, pour the soup over and serve, handing the cheese separately.

TIPS AND VARIATIONS-
- alternatively put the *croûtes* on top of the soup in individual bowls, sprinkle the cheese over and put under a hot grill for a few minutes until bubbling and golden
- stock cubes or chicken stock are acceptable substitutes
- cheddar is fine if you have no *gruyère* or parmesan

GAZPACHO ANDALUZ

*There are umpteen different recipes for this classic Spanish cold soup,
but this one is really excellent, and made perfect by the garnishes*

500g ripe tomatoes

400g can of tomato juice

1 large Spanish onion

2 large red peppers

¾ cucumber

2-4 cloves garlic

4 thickish slices fairly stale white bread

olive oil

2 dsps red wine vinegar

seasoning

NOTES

FOR THE GARNISH

2 slices white bread

2 large ripe tomatoes

¼ cucumber

small red and green peppers

2 hard boiled eggs

bunch of spring onions

Process the bread into crumbs and put into a large bowl. Stir in the vinegar and add as much olive oil as they will absorb, probably 4-6 tbs.

Skin and roughly chop the tomatoes. Coarsely chop the onion, cucumber and peppers. Crush the garlic. Put into a blender and gradually add most of the tomato juice.

Stir the salad mixture into the bowl with the breadcrumbs and chill until ready to serve.

Prepare the garnish. Each item should be presented separately in individual bowls. Skin and deseed the tomatoes and cucumbers and cut into small cubes. Similarly dice the peppers and the eggs. Slice into small rings the white part of the spring onions. Finally, cut the bread into small cubes and fry in butter to make crisp *croûtons*.

Add some ice cubes to the chilled soup and serve handing round the various garnishes.

TIPS AND VARIATIONS-

- use more or less tomato juice to get your preferred consistency
- apart from the fried bread *croûtons*, everything can be done well in advance

LEEK AND CHICKPEA SOUP

We were first served this soup on a cold day's woodcock
shooting in Anglesey and thought it quite delicious - so here it is

4-6 leeks   NOTES

200g chickpeas

3-4 cloves garlic

butter

150g parmesan cheese

2 pints chicken stock

seasoning

parsley

Soak the chickpeas overnight and then simmer in fresh water until cooked and tender.

Clean the leeks and slice into smallish strips. Slice the garlic cloves. Grate the parmesan but keep a few shavings for garnish.

Gently heat a large heavy pan, melt some butter and stir the garlic for a minute or two. Add the leeks, stir to coat with butter, cover and simmer gently for 15-20 minutes until the leeks are softened.

Add the chickpeas and 1 pint of stock and bring to a simmer. Use a hand held blender to liquidise about three quarters of the soup; or to whatever consistency you prefer.

Add the rest of the stock, the grated parmesan and season to taste. Cover and simmer for 20 minutes or so.

Serve very hot garnished with parmesan shavings and chopped parsley.

TIPS AND VARIATIONS-
- use tinned chickpeas if you prefer
- you can liquidise it completely if you prefer as smooth soup

PORTUGUESE CABBAGE SOUP

*A substantial peasant soup with a delicious flavour that
improves on reheating and can easily be a meal in itself*

1 medium Savoy cabbage	NOTES
500g potatoes	
500g smoked sausages	
2 medium/large onions	
2 medium carrots	
3-4 garlic cloves	
olive oil and butter	
350ml chicken stock	
2 tins tomatoes	
200g red kidney beans	
salt and pepper	

Simmer the beans in slightly salted water for 20-30 minutes until just cooked, then drain.

Prick the sausages and blanch in boiling water briefly to release the fat. Drain and cut into slices.

Cut the cabbage diagonally into wide slices. Cut the potato into chunks. Coarsely chop one onion, slice the other, chop the carrots and crush the garlic.

In a large pan gently *sauté* the potatoes, onions, carrots and garlic for a few minutes in oil and butter. Add the stock and simmer, covered, for 20 minutes or so until the potatoes are just cooked. Mash some of the potatoes against the side of the pan – this will thicken the soup –

Stir in the tomatoes, kidney beans, cabbage and the sausage. Season and simmer for 15-20 minutes until everything is just cooked.

TIPS AND VARIATIONS-

* use chorizo or similar spicy sausage
* the flavour is much enhanced if the soup is made beforehand and gently reheated
* stock cubes are good enough, but try a genuinely made stock and taste the difference
* individual quantities in this sort of recipe are not too important
* use tinned red beans if this is easier

POTAGE BONNE FEMME

*This simple 'country' soup is the basic method from which most good vegetable soups are created;
the most important part being the absorption of butter by the vegetables*

2 large leeks
2 large carrots
500g potatoes
2 sticks celery
125g butter
1 litre water
seasoning
chopped parsley

NOTES

Clean and slice the leeks, using only the white part. Coarsely chop the potatoes, carrots and the celery.

In a large heavy pan and over a gentle heat, melt the butter, then stir in the vegetables. Cover and cook slowly for 5-10 minutes, stirring occasionally, until the butter is absorbed.

Add the water and seasoning, cover, and simmer gently for 30 minutes or so, until the vegetables are just tender. Remove from the heat and let cool a little.

Liquidise in a blender until smooth. Reheat gently and serve with the parsley scattered on top.

TIPS AND VARIATIONS-

* use stock instead of water for a richer taste
* liquidise only half so you have lumpy bits floating around
* decorate with a swirl of cream
* this reheats very well
* if you press through a sieve, which is what one did before blenders were invented, you will have an even smoother and more sophisticated soup

RUSSIAN CUCUMBER
AND SPINACH SOUP

An easily made but rather sumptuous first course; an ideal starter before a summer barbeque

500g spinach

400ml single cream

400ml plain yoghurt

800ml (2 tins) consommé

1 cucumber

4 eggs

2 handfuls chives,
fennel fronds or tarragon

seasoning and lemon juice to taste

NOTES

Wash and coarsely chop the spinach – put in a large pan and stir, covered, over a moderate heat, for a few minutes until wilted.

Peel and deseed the cucumber and chop into small pieces. Hard boil the eggs and coarsely chop the yolks and whites separately. Chop the herbs.

When the spinach is cold add all the other ingredients in the order as above. Gently stir into a large bowl or soup tureen and season to taste. Chill for several hours.

VARIATIONS AND TIPS-

- if you can, use sorrel instead of spinach; this gives a more authentic version
- reserve some chopped egg yolk and herbs to garnish
- the best *consommés* will set to a firmish gelatinous texture
- will keep in the fridge for two or three days

VICHYSSOISE

A classic soup and a great standby when you have a surfeit of leeks in the vegetable garden

750g leeks
750g potatoes
100g butter
1 litre water
seasoning
crème fraîche
chopped parsley

Clean the leeks and, using only the white parts chop them and the potatoes into large chunks.

Melt the butter in a large pan, put in the vegetables and stir, covered, over a gentle heat until the butter is absorbed, about 10-15 minutes.

Add the water and seasoning, cover and simmer gently for 15-20 minutes, until the vegetables are just cooked.

Liquidise and serve garnished with the *crème fraîche* and parsley.

TIPS AND VARIATIONS-

* using chicken stock instead of water makes a richer soup
* pass through a sieve to make a more delicate version
* reserve some of the vegetable chunks and add after liquidising
* use a hand held liquidiser for a more rustic version and to save time
* add a few bits of chopped ham

HORS D'OEUVRE

A Salad of Carrot and Onion
An Orangey Crab Salad
Asparagus Dishes
Céleri-ravé rémoulade
Champignons à la Grècque
Cheesey little gems
Ensaladilla
Fenouils à la Grècque
Glazed Turnips
Tomates accordéon
Hors d'oeuvre à la Moulin
Moules Marinière and Variations
Roasted red Peppers
Stuffed Courgette flowers with Sage leaves
Tricolore

AN INTERESTING PHRASE, literally meaning 'outside the main work', *hors d'oeuvre* was originally an architectural term referring to an outbuilding that was not a part of the main design; later borrowed by French chefs to describe a dish 'outside' the main course of a meal.

The French idea of 'interesting' little first courses, either on their own or in combination, is one of the pleasures of planning and preparing a meal. The range of possibilities and opportunity for complementary combinations of taste, colour and texture is always a decision making challenge. The ideas here just happen to be some of my favourites.

Of course many national cuisines do this - tapas, mezes, antipasta, etc; but none so effectively as the French - think of the appetising displays in every provincial charcuterie. What they all have in common is that there are nearly always only one or two, usually vegetable, ingredients treated with respect and cooked with care. Many of these dishes can be used as vegetable accompaniments, and of course, vice versa."

I always rather liked the observation from Saki's 'Reginald at the Carlton' - "*Hors d'oeuvres* have always had a pathetic interest for me; they remind me of going through childhood and youth wondering what the next course will bring – and during the rest of the menu one wishes one had eaten more of the *hors d'oeuvres*".

A SALAD OF CARROT AND ONION

This simple salad is a useful hors d'oeuvre and goes rather well with spicy dishes

5-6 young carrots

bunch spring onions

juice of half a lemon

seasoning

1tbs olive oil

fresh ginger

¼ tsp cayenne pepper

any green herbs

Clean the carrots and cut into *julienne* strips, preferably on the diagonal. Finely slice the onions into thin ringlets. Finely chop the herbs.

Put the carrots into a large pan of boiling salted water, bring back to the boil, remove almost immediately, and drain. Rinse under cold running water and drain again.

Combine and toss together the carrots, onions, lemon juice, olive oil, seasoning and cayenne. Finely grate a little ginger over the salad mixture and decorate with some chopped green herbs.

Tips and Variations-

- you could use very thinly sliced shallots or just an ordinary onion
- the carrots need to be just *al dente; y*ou must use your judgement here
- the salad will keep for some time and can be served at room temperature or cold
- if you prefer, whisk the oil and lemon juice into a dressing first

AN ORANGEY CRAB SALAD

*The taste of crab and the orange combine beautifully in this attractive
and easily made starter which can be prepared well in advance*

250g crabmeat   NOTES

1 orange

½ tsp Dijon mustard

2tsp white wine vinegar

6tbs olive oil

seasoning

handful parsley

4 slices wholemeal bread

Grate the zest from the orange and squeeze out the juice. Chop the parsley.

Make a dressing by whisking together the oil, vinegar, orange juice, mustard, zest and seasoning to taste.

Put the crabmeat in a bowl, add 2 tbs of the dressing and mix well together.

Place a 2½" round pastry cutter onto a serving plate and put in one quarter of the crabmeat mixture. Gently firm up with the back of a teaspoon. Carefully remove the cutter leaving a neat round of crab. Repeat on three other plates.

To serve, drizzle half the remaining orange dressing round each plate and scatter over the parsley. Toast the bread and cut into 'soldiers'. Dip each soldier into the remaining dressing and eat with a little crab.

TIPS AND VARIATIONS-

- use about 50/50 brown and white crabmeat, but if more white the better
- the dressed crab will keep for several hours in the fridge
- try using an Italian bread such as focaccia or ciabatta

ASPARAGUS DISHES

The climate and soil in certain parts of England are the only places in the world that grow really top quality asparagus, and the season is all too short – 6-7 weeks in May and June – make the most of it

Basic perfection- simmer a bunch of asparagus in salted water for 5-6 minutes, until *al dente*, drain, and serve with melted butter and lemon slices. Eat with your fingers.

Asparagus Vinaigrette- cook as above, allow to cool and serve with a french dressing.

Asparagus Omelette- cook as above, cool under the tap and cut into ½" pieces. Lightly beat 5-6 eggs in a bowl, fold in the asparagus with some grated parmesan, sea salt, pepper, and chopped chives and oregano. Heat gently a little olive oil and butter in a wide lidded pan and pour in the mixture. Let it cook for a few minutes, drawing in the edges with a spatula, then cover and continue to cook for 5 minutes or so until the top is just set. Serve in wedges with a little more grated cheese and herbs scattered on top.

Stir fried Asparagus- cut into 1" lengths. In a lidded wok, or wide pan, heat some olive oil until smoking hot. Add the asparagus and stir fry for 2-3 minutes. Season with sea salt and freshly ground pepper and add 4tbs water. Cover and cook over a more gentle heat for a few minutes until the asparagus is just tender. You could add some frozen petit pois with the water.

Tuna, pasta and asparagus salad- dust tuna steaks with ground cumin and coriander, or other spices, and chargrill for 2-3 minutes each side and break into pieces. Cook some attractive looking pasta shapes. Stir fry a bunch of asparagus as above. Make a salad of little gem lettuces and french dressing with lots of finely chopped ginger, then gently toss everything together. Add thinly sliced red pepper for more colour.

Whitsun Lamb- a delicious combination of asparagus tips, sauce from the stalks and spring lamb – see page 103.

TIPS AND VARIATIONS-

- bending an asparagus stalk in half will break it at exactly the right point to remove the fibrous part
- rinse before cooking to remove any dirt
- the flavour is best when freshest, but is okay for 24 hours in the fridge or water
- imported out of season asparagus is not the same at all
- hollandaise sauce is a good alternative to butter
- if you see asparagus for sale just buy it, don't ask when you are going to eat it – you will
- never overcook, unless you want to make a soup – remember the tips will cook much faster than the body of the stalk
- use as a vegetable accompaniment to grilled meat dishes

CÉLERI-RAVÉ RÉMOULADE

Celeriac with mustard mayonnaise – a favourite of mine

1 celeriac

lemon juice

2-3 tbs mayonnaise

1 tsp dijon mustard

parsley

bunch of spring onions

1 tsp capers or a gherkin

NOTES

Peel the celeriac and cut into thin 'chip' sized strips and immediately put into a bowl of water acidulated with lemon juice, as otherwise it browns very quickly. Finely chop the onions, parsley and the gherkins or capers.

Drain the celeriac, then plunge into boiling salted water and blanch for two to three minutes until just *al dente*. Drain, rinse under cold water and drain again. Put into a large bowl.

Mix the mustard, parsley, onion and gherkin into the mayonnaise and dilute with a little olive oil, or hot water, to a thinnish coating consistency. Stir a sufficient amount into the celeriac to lightly coat. Decorate with a little more parsley. Cool for an hour or two.

TIPS AND VARIATIONS-
- take care not to overcook the celeriac – a useful little tip is that the greater the volume of water, the more quickly it comes back to the boil
- mix with freshly cooked mussels *–Moules à la Fécampoise* – this is absolutely delicious, or try it with prawns or chopped king prawns
- serve as part of a mixed *hors d'oeuvre*
- will keep for two or three days in the fridge
- add some thinly sliced strips of salami or mortadella

CHAMPIGNONS À LA GRÈCQUE

A simple and delicate little stand by starter dish with many attractive variations

400g button mushrooms
5 tbs olive oil
5 tbs white wine
1 tbs lemon juice
2 tbs chopped onion
3 tsps tomato purée
bay leaf
seasoning
parsley

NOTES

Put everything except the mushrooms and parsley into a pan and simmer for 5-10 minutes.

Add the button mushrooms (if large cut into halves or quarters) – cover and simmer for

10 minutes or so, stirring occasionally, until only just cooked.

Remove the mushrooms and arrange in a shallow dish. Reduce the liquid to a syrupy consistency by boiling for a few minutes. Then pour over the mushrooms.

Chill and serve, garnished with chopped parsley, as part of a mixed *hors d'oeuvre*, or, as a starter, on its own.

TIPS AND VARIATIONS-

- try this with a other salad vegetables – eg. courgettes, leeks, french beans etc. – most will need cooking rather longer– see recipe for *fenouil à la grècque* page 23
- add chopped garlic to spice it up a bit
- will keep for several days in the fridge

CHEESEY LITTLE GEMS

*A rather surprising and simple lettuce dish that goes well with any grilled or barbequed meat ,
but is also very good as an hors d'oeuvre in its own right - a great combination of taste and texture*

3-4 little gem lettuces

200g stilton cheese

3tbs crème fraîche

NOTES

Cut the cheese into little pieces and put into a small pan with the *crème fraîche*. Cook very gently over a very low heat, stirring constantly, until the cheese has melted and there are no lumpy bits left. Remove and allow to cool.

Meanwhile remove the outer leaves from the little gem lettuces. Halve them lengthwise and then, depending on their size, halve again or quarter. The stem should hold each section together.

Arrange the lettuce pieces closely together on a serving dish, or on individual plates; pour over the cheese sauce and serve.

TIPS AND VARIATIONS-

- any reasonable blue cheese will do perfectly well
- also very good after a main course and before the pudding
- equally good with the cheese sauce still warm or completely cool

ENSALADILLA

A pretty and attractive looking 'tapas' starter or part of a mixed hors d'oeuvre

750g new or waxy potatoes   NOTES
2 medium sized young carrots
250g prawns
150ml mayonnaise
seasoning
parsley

Boil the potatoes until just cooked. When cool chop and dice them into very small pieces.

Boil the carrots until just cooked, rinse in cold water and again cut into small dice.

Peel and coarsely chop the prawns. Mix with the potatoes and carrots. Fold in enough mayonnaise, thinned if necessary with a little warm water, to lightly coat the ingredients.

Pile up and serve, garnished with chopped parsley or any green herb.

TIPS AND VARIATIONS-
- this simple dish takes care - it should look like egg mayonnaise, not potato salad
- the potatoes must be firm and diced, not crumbled
- the quality of the ingredients, especially the prawns, makes a critical difference
- you could add a few chopped green beans or little peas
- will keep for two or three days in the fridge

FENOUILS À LA GRECQUE
An unusually aromatic variation on this method of cooking vegetables

2 good size fennel heads

2-3 bunches of spring onions

2 tbs tomato purée

60g sultanas

2 tbs olive oil

seasoning

1 tsp dried mixed herbs

½ tsp ground coriander

½ tsp cayenne pepper

1 bay leaf

1 glass dry white wine

NOTES

Trim the fennel heads and cut into quarters or smaller depending on their size. Finely chop the onions.

Put the oil into a wide pan, add the fennel and onion, and *sauté* gently for 10-15 minutes, until beginning to soften.

Add the tomato *purée*, seasoning, herbs, spices, bay leaf and wine, stir and cover, and simmer very gently for 30-40 minutes – half way through add the sultanas - until the fennel is tender.

If the mixture is too liquid, uncover for a while towards the end.

TIPS AND VARIATIONS-

- very good hot or cold, or as part of a mixed *hors d'oeuvre*
- the fennel needs to be tender and always takes longer than one thinks; you could blanch it first to speed things up
- use sliced onions and/or fresh herbs if you wish
- the liquid should end up as a thick concentrate of oil, wine and tomato – keep reducing until you achieve this

GLAZED TURNIPS

These navets glacés are delicious hot or cold (if you like turnips) and good
as part of a mixed hors d'oeuvre or could be an accompaniment to a roast

500g young turnips

3 tsps castor sugar

50g butter

NOTES

Peel the turnips which should be about the size of a good strawberry. Cut larger ones into pieces

Gently boil in lightly salted water until only just tender. Drain, but leave 2-3 tbs of water in the pan.

Add the sugar and butter and over a gentle heat stir around until it caramelises and a sticky glaze is formed. Remove the turnips and spoon the glaze over to serve.

TIPS AND VARIATIONS-
- this also works with button onions, shallots or mushrooms.
- take care not to overcook

TOMATES ACCORDÉON

A very simple hors d'oeuvre that just looks rather pretty

4 ripe beef tomatoes

4 large eggs

mayonnaise

parsley

NOTES

Hard boil the eggs. When cool, peel and cut longways into thin slices. Chop the parsley.

Put the tomatoes, stem down, onto a chopping board and slice vertically almost to the base. Open each one out – like a concertina – put a slice of egg between each tomato slice.

Arrange on individual plates or a serving dish and spoon over each a dessertspoonful of mayonnaise. Sprinkle over the parsley.

TIPS AND VARIATIONS–
- instead of parsley use chopped olives or chives

HORS D'OEUVRE À LA MOULIN

I include this only because it was one of our earliest experiences of how good a very simple but well presented french salad dish can be and the Moulin near Duras was for some years, quite our favourite place to eat in the whole of France

½ a white cabbage

500g waxy potatoes

2 eggs

bunch of spring onions

parsley

a very garlicky french dressing

coarsely ground black pepper

NOTES

Boil the potatoes until just cooked and when cool cut into ½" cubes. Finely slice the cabbage and blanch for 4-5 minutes. Hard boil and shell the eggs. Chop the spring onions.

Separately dress the cabbage and the potatoes. Quarter the egg whites and mash the yolks. Chop the parsley.

Arrange the cabbage around the outside of an *entrée* dish. Mix the potatoes and spring onions together and pile in the middle. Decorate with the egg whites and scatter over the parsley, egg yolks and black pepper.

TIPS AND VARIATIONS—

- there are of course an infinity of variations, but this was the original

MOULES MARINIÈRE AND VARIATIONS

*A classic dish well worth the time taken in cleaning
the mussels and with several excellent variations*

1kg bag of mussels   NOTES
medium onion
2 glasses dry white wine
black pepper
handful of parsley

Clean the mussels in running water, discarding any that are broken or dead. Chop finely the onion and parsley.

Put everything into a large pan, cover and cook over a medium heat for 5-6 minutes, shaking the pan gently from time to time, until the mussels have opened.

Serve in a large bowl with plenty of french bread to mop up the juices.

TIPS AND VARIATIONS—

* it is most important that the mussels are properly cleaned and the beards removed
* it is very easy to overcook which shrivels up and spoils the mussels
* very good cold too
* remove the mussels when done and reduce the liquid with butter or cream to make a richer dish
* add the mussels to a fish pie or use to decorate any plain fish dish
* add a tin of tomatoes when cooking and remove the mussels from their shells when done, for a tasty mussel soup
* remove mussels from shells and add to *celeri-ravi remoulade*, see page 19, to make *'moules à la fécampoise'* - delicious
* make a simple curry sauce with ginger, garlic, onions and a few ground spices, and then cook the mussels in this

ROASTED RED PEPPERS

Looks superb – tastes brilliant – made in moments

3 large red peppers
6 cherry tomatoes
10 anchovy fillets
3 cloves garlic
olive oil
black pepper
basil

NOTES

Cut the peppers in half and remove the seeds and pith, but leave on the stalks. Halve the tomatoes. Chop the garlic finely and cut the anchovies in half.

Put the pepper halves, open side up, in a lightly oiled roasting tin. Into each pepper put 2 tomato halves, and the garlic and anchovies divided equally. Drizzle olive oil generously over each pepper and season with black pepper.

Put the roasting tray into a medium hot oven, c.190°C, and cook for 40-50 minutes until the peppers are just soft and blackening round the edges.

Transfer to a serving dish, pour over the pan juices and decorate with shredded basil leaves.

TIPS AND VARIATIONS-

- make sure you have plenty of bread to mop up the delicious juices
- leave the stalks on the peppers as it makes them look more attractive
- use a shallow roasting tin which helps toast the pepper edges
- to be even more perfect, skin the tomatoes by covering with boiling water for 40 seconds – the skins will then just slip off

STUFFED COURGETTE FLOWERS
WITH SAGE LEAVES

I believe this recipe comes from Italy – really you can only try it if you grow your own courgettes – it's pretty fiddly and very much a last minute thing to do with friends. But it does look very pretty!

10 courgette flowers   NOTES
15 sage leaves
100g plain flour
1 egg
200ml beer
100g gruyère cheese
sunflower oil
seasoning

Make a batter by putting the flour into a food processor with the egg and mixing briefly; gradually mix in the beer and add the seasoning.

Cut the gruyère into small cubes and insert one or two inside each courgette flower.

Heat enough oil to deep fry, until smoking hot. Put the batter into a bowl.

Dip the stuffed flowers in the batter and then immediately into the hot oil until a light golden colour. You may have to do this in two or three batches. Lay on absorbent kitchen paper to drain.

Put all the sage leaves into the batter and then fry them similarly until slightly brown and crisp. Pile the leaves and flowers up together on a warm dish and serve at once.

TIPS AND VARIATIONS-
- choose flowers that are closed rather than open
- courgette flowers, rather like those on chives, have a lot of colourful taste and can be used to decorate all sorts of salad and other dishes
- goat's cheese is good too

TRICOLORE

An attractive and colourful salad, so called, because the
red, white and green resemble the Italian national flag

ripe avocado pears

mozzarella cheese

beef tomatoes

olive oil and lemon juice

sea salt and freshly ground pepper

basil leaves

NOTES

Peel the tomatoes and avocado. Cut them and the mozzarella into even slices.

Arrange avocado, cheese and tomato slices in stripes across individual plates or a serving dish.

Sprinkle over the oil and lemon juice and scatter with the shredded basil leaves and seasoning.

TIPS AND VARIATIONS-

* buffalo mozzarella is of course the best
* if you have the time, marinate the cheese slices in a dressing of the oil and lemon juice for a few hours beforehand – this really enhances the flavour
* chives or any other fresh green herb could replace the basil
* you could make a *purée* of the avocado and arrange the tomatoes and cheese slices around this
* peel tomatoes by putting into very hot water for 40 seconds – the skin will then just slip off

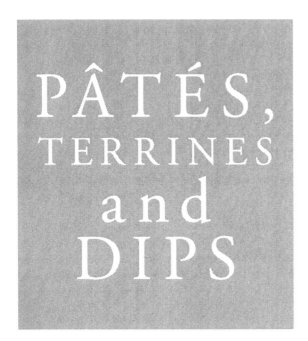

PÂTÉS,
TERRINES
and
DIPS

A simple Tuna Fish Pâté
Smoked Mackerel Pâté
Aubergine purée
Brawn
Herb Terrine
Herring Roe Pâté
Hoummus
Mushroom Pâté
Pâté De Campagne
Pheasant Terrine
Scallop And Salmon Rillettes
Terrine of Skate
Tzatziki
Vegetable Terrine

THESE WONDERFUL DISHES offer immense scope for imaginative and creative cooking. Not for nothing are pâté and terrine both French words and every charcuterie and bistro will have its own terrine du chef or pâté maison. Strictly speaking a terrine is the dish in which a pâté is cooked, but I tend to think of a pâté as being smooth and sophisticated and a terrine being more coarse and rustic in texture.

Whilst belly pork, liver, fat and meat may be thought of as standard ingredients, pâtés of fish and vegetables can have a delicacy of taste and texture and a prettiness that can make them irresistible. Dips too can be such a useful standby accompaniment or just great with a few sliced raw vegetables.

One of their big advantages is that they can all be made well in advance and kept in the fridge for several days. In fact generally, though not with fish, the flavour improves over time. They can all be served on their own or as part of a mixed *hors d'oeuvre*.

Terrines are usually cooked in the oven in a *bain mairie* which is simply a baking tin, half filled with hot water, in which the terrine dish stands to ensure slow, moist and even cooking in gentle heat.

A VERY SIMPLE TUNA FISH PÂTÉ

A rapidly made starter for emergencies

1 tin of tuna
100g unsalted butter
juice of half a lemon
a few fresh herbs
black pepper

Put everything into an electric blender and mix at a medium speed until all is very smooth.

Turn into individual pots and chill. Serve with thin 'soldiers' of hot toast.

TIPS AND VARIATIONS-

*   tinned salmon is good too
*   decorate with sliced olives or cucumber
*   will keep for several days in the fridge

SMOKED MACKEREL PÂTÉ

Also quick and easily made but rather more subtle

2-3 fillets smoked mackerel
juice of half a lemon
1-3tsps horseradish sauce
250g crème fraîche
nutmeg and seasoning

Remove the skin and flake the fish. Put into a mixing bowl with the lemon juice, horseradish and *crème fraîche*. Season to taste and grate in some nutmeg.

Gently stir all together and spoon into individual ramekins. Chill. Serve with pieces of melba toast and unsalted butter.

TIPS AND VARIATIONS-

*   horseradish varies hugely in strength – especially homemade – take care not to overdo it!
*   instead of *crème fraîche* try cream cheese, greek yoghurt or soured cream
*   you could add a little chopped parsley

AUBERGINE PURÉE

The soft and silky texture of this savoury purée has a slightly smoky taste

2 good aubergines
1-2 fat garlic cloves
3tbs olive oil
juice of a lemon
seasoning
parsley or coriander

NOTES

Bake the aubergines in a hot oven for 35-45 minutes or so until soft. Scrape the flesh from the skin and put in a blender.

Crush the garlic with a little salt, chop the herbs and add to the aubergine in the blender with the oil, lemon juice and pepper to taste.

Liquidise at top speed until reduced a smooth paste. Chill for 2-3 hours.

Serve with pitta bread, black olives and hard boiled eggs.

TIPS AND VARIATIONS-

* if the aubergine seeds are a problem then push through a sieve
* serve as part of a mixed *hors d'oeuvre* or use as a dip for raw vegetables
* vary the flavour by adding a little onion, curry paste or yoghurt
* add an egg yolk to make it a little richer
* you could serve this with lamb meatballs and minted yoghurt

BRAWN

*Not everybody's cup of tea, this; it's a very messy thing to do, but if you're
feeling a little ambitious, the end result is really very tasty – very cheap too!*

½ a pig's head   NOTES
large onion
2-3 carrots and celery sticks
1tsp peppercorns
bouquet garni
salt and pepper

The head must first be soaked in brine for several hours or overnight – so put 2-3 tablespoons salt
into a large enough pan, half fill with water and stir around. Put in the head and just cover with
more water.

When you are ready, wash the head well, put back into the pan and just cover with fresh water. Add
the roughly chopped onion, carrot and celery together with the peppercorns and bouquet.

Cover the pan and bring to the boil. Simmer gently, either on top of the stove or in the oven, for 2½
-3½ hours until the meat comes easily from the bone.

Lift out the head. Strain the stock and let it boil for a while to reduce. Cool and put in the fridge.

Remove all the meat from the head; the tongue and cheeks will be the largest bits; pull and shred it
all into small pieces. Discard the bones, the fatty bits, gristle and skin etc. Pack all the meat pieces
into a 2½ pint terrine, peppering liberally.

Skim off as much fat as possible from the reduced stock and use to moisten the meat so it is just
covered.

Chill overnight, turn out of the terrine, and serve by cutting into very thin slices with the following
dressing:-

Dressing for brawn – whisk well together; 2 tbs brown sugar, 3 tbs cider vinegar, 6tbs oil, 1tsp made
mustard, salt, pepper and a pinch of nutmeg.

TIPS AND VARIATIONS-

- if the stock has set well it should be possible to turn the brawn out of the terrine quite
  easily using a sharp knife – or put into a very hot oven for a few moments first
- if you line the terrine with clingfilm it will turn out easily
- most butchers can get you a pig's head, usually for free and £1 in the charity box
- taste the stock at some stage – it may need more salt
- try this recipe using oxtail instead of the pig's head – not bad!

A HERB TERRINE

A delightful green flecked and rough textured herb flavoured country terrine

500g spinach
500g lean belly pork
150g cooked ham
2 handfuls fresh herbs
medium onion
2 cloves garlic
1-2 slices of bread
seasoning
grated nutmeg
1 egg
4 rashers streaky bacon

NOTES

Quickly blanch the spinach in boiling salted water, and squeeze or press in a sieve, to get it as dry as possible. Chop the herbs.

Mince the pork. Then put through the mincer the spinach, the onion, the garlic and finally the bread. Dice the ham. Mix all these together with the chopped herbs, egg and seasonings and stir very thoroughly.

Pack into a 2½ pint terrine dish and dome the top – spread the stretched bacon over and let stand for the flavours to amalgamate for a few hours. Put in a *bain marie*, cover, and cook for 60 minutes or so in a medium oven.

Cool and mature for 24 hours in the fridge. Serve by slicing from the terrine.

TIPS AND VARIATIONS-

* garnish with herbs and olives
* parsley, oregano, tarragon, chives, basil , marjoram, etc – whatever is available
* vary the quantities of garlic and other herbs to taste

HERRING ROE PÂTÉ

A very rich, unusual and rather piquant fish pâté

250g soft herring roes
juice of a half lemon
knob of butter
6 anchovy fillets
4 tbs double cream
1 tsp capers
seasoning

NOTES

Season the herring roes, add the lemon juice and leave for a few minutes. Whip the cream and chop the capers.

Drain the roes. Heat the butter in a pan until foaming, add the roes and cook for a few moments only until they curl and firm up.

Blend gently in a food processor with the pan juices and the anchovy fillets. Cool.

Fold the whipped cream into the mixture along with the capers. Chill and serve.

TIPS AND VARIATIONS-
- use only very fresh roes
- as this is so rich use as an *hors d'oeuvre* on little biscuits dusted with cayenne
- take care not to overcook the roes, which are very delicate

HOUMMUS

There are many variations on making hoummus but this recipe works very well.
It has to be planned well in advance to allow the chickpeas time to soak and cook

200g chickpeas

reserved cooking liquor

juice of ½-1 small lemon

2-3 large garlic cloves

1 tbs tahini paste

olive oil

sea salt and cayenne pepper

chopped parsley to garnish

NOTES

Soak the chickpeas overnight and then simmer in fresh water until tender – this can take an hour or two. Strain them and reserve the cooking liquor.

Put a few tablespoons of the liquor into a blender with the lemon juice and garlic and blend a little - then slowly add the chick peas and tahini. If the mixture seems too thick add some olive oil and perhaps more liquor.

You should end up with a thick, beige and slightly gritty *purée*. Check the taste carefully, add a little salt and cayenne, and decide whether to add more garlic, oil or lemon juice.

Put into a bowl, spread a thin layer of olive oil over the surface and chill.

TIPS AND VARIATIONS-
- the chickpeas almost double their weight after soaking and cooking – you can substitute 400g of a ready tinned or bottled variety – saves a lot of time
- make a greater quantity of chickpeas to use in other dishes such as falafel
- tahini is easily made by dry roasting sesame seeds, grinding finely and mixing with olive oil to form a thick oily paste
- hoummus will keep for several days in the fridge
- the taste and consistency can be varied to one's preference by the amount of garlic, oil, lemon juice used - the garlic is raw so quite fierce!
- serve with buttered toast or as part of a mixed *hôrs d'oeuvre*

MUSHROOM PÂTÉ

An easily made starter or part of a mixed hôrs d'oeuvre

400g mushrooms
medium onion
butter
150g breadcrumbs
100ml hot water
juice of ½ lemon
2 garlic cloves
ground nutmeg and seasoning

NOTES

Finely chop the mushrooms and the onion. Crush and very finely chop the garlic.

Melt a little butter in a pan and *sauté* the onion until soft, then add the mushrooms and stir for a few minutes only. Do not let the mushrooms start to go mushy. It should be quite dry.

Soak the breadcrumbs in the hot water and then add to the mushrooms with the lemon juice and garlic. Cook very gently, stirring for a few minutes longer until any liquid is absorbed. Add the nutmeg and seasoning to taste.

Put onto a serving dish, let it cool and chill until required. Garnish with very thinly sliced raw mushroom and parsley.

TIPS AND VARIATIONS-

- use the 'closed cap' mushrooms which are firmer
- although quick and easy to make it is important to get the garlic, onion and mushrooms cooked to the right consistency – it should be dry and not juicy
- it may be easier to not soak the breadcrumbs, but add enough water later to get the right consistency

PÂTÉ DE CAMPAGNE

A savoury rough textured country terrine that keeps well (and indeed improves)
for several days in the fridge – this is my favourite

250g pie veal   NOTES

400g belly pork

250g pigs liver

150g ham- in a piece

3 cloves garlic

150g back pork fat – diced roughly

seasonings

1tsp allspice

medium onion

chopped parsley or tarragon

thick slice of bread

4 tbs brandy, or white wine

3-4 rashers thin streaky bacon

2-3 bay leaves

Coarsely mince the veal, belly pork and liver. Then put through the mincer, the onion, garlic, allspice and finally the bread – which cleans through the juices.

Mix together very thoroughly with the diced back pork fat, brandy, seasonings and chopped herbs. Cut the ham into ½" strips.

Line a 2½ pint terrine dish with the bacon so that most of it can be folded back over the top. Fill the terrine with the mixture putting the strips of ham in layers through the middle. Fold over the bacon and put the bay leaves on top. Cover and let stand for an hour or two.

Place the covered terrine in a baking tray with hot water halfway up (a *bain-marie*) and cook in a moderate oven, c.180°C, for about 1½ hours. Let it cool and then mature in the fridge overnight or even a day or two.

TIPS AND VARIATIONS-
* the diced back fat gives lovely white blobs throughout
* quantities can be varied significantly to taste
* allow to reach room temperature before serving
* serve by cutting thick slices on a slant
* if pie veal is unavailable, skinless chicken breast can substitute

PHEASANT TERRINE

When pheasants are virtually two a penny this is a splendid way to make good use of them

1 pheasant
250g fresh belly pork
1tbs cooking brandy
125g pig's liver
2tbs Madeira (or sherry)
juice of a half orange
½ a medium onion
chopped herbs
2 cloves garlic
4 rashers thin streaky bacon
seasoning
slice of bread

NOTES

Remove the flesh from the pheasant and the rind and bone from the belly pork.

Put both meats through the mincer followed by the liver. Coarsely chop the onion and garlic and mince these with the herbs. Finally mince the bread and mix everything together.

Add the brandy, Madeira, orange juice and seasoning. Mix very well and leave to marinate in the fridge for a few hours or overnight.

Line a 2½ pint terrine dish with the bacon rashers and pack in the mixture so that some of the bacon can be folded back over the top. Cover, and put the terrine in a baking tin half filled with hot water, a *bain marie*. Cook in a moderate oven, c.180°C, for about 1½ hours.

Allow to cool and mature in the fridge for a day or two.

TIPS AND VARIATIONS-
- if pheasants are really plentiful just use the breasts
- you can use duck, pigeon or other game
- use the remaining carcase to make stock
- mincing the bread helps clean the mincer and adds a little body

SCALLOP AND SALMON RILLETTES

An easily made starter or even a little 'mise en bouche'

8 fresh scallops
250g salmon fillet, skin on
1-2tbs crème fraîche
glass of white wine
½ a medium onion
pepper
parsley

NOTES

Take the skin off the salmon. Put it, the skin that is, in a saucepan with the wine, about a pint of water and the chopped onion. Simmer for 15-20 minutes to make a simple *court bouillon*. Strain and let it cool a little.

Put the skinned salmon fillet into a shallow pan filled with just enough *court bouillon* to cover. Cover and simmer very gently for five or six minutes until the salmon is barely cooked. Remove and let it cool.

Put the scallops into the *court bouillon,* poach for only a minute or two, and remove – again they should be practically raw in the middle.

Using two forks on a chopping board pull the salmon flesh apart along the grain – rather like shredding Peking duck! Cut the scallops into small dice.

When cooled, season both with a little pepper and mix all together very loosely with just enough of the *crème fraîche* to bind it together. Chill for an hour or two.

Serve in individual ramekins with a little chopped parsley.

TIPS AND VARIATIONS-
- never use scallops that have been frozen – they lose all their delicious flavour
- you could use cream or yoghourt instead of *crème fraîche*
- remember both scallops and salmon will cook for a little longer when removed from the liquid

TERRINE OF SKATE

*This works well with skate because it is naturally gelatinous
and, unlike most fish, keeps a lot of flavour when cold*

COURT BOUILLON INGREDIENTS-   NOTES

½ bottle dry white wine

2 pints water

bay leaf

seasoning

chopped medium onion

sliced carrot

chopped celery stick

slice of lemon

1kg skate wings

bunch of spring onions

a handful of parsley

seasoning

10g sachet gelatine powder

Make a *court bouillon* in a wide shallow pan by simmering all the ingredients together, covered, for 20-25 minutes. Strain and put in the skate wing. Cover and simmer gently for 8-10 minutes. Lift the fish out and let it cool.

Strain the stock into a clean pan and boil vigorously until reduced to about one pint. Let it cool.

Sprinkle the gelatine powder over a little cold water in a pan and stir into the reduced stock.

Gently remove the flesh from the skate, pulling it apart a little. Finely chop the spring onions and parsley and mix in a bowl with the skate and a little seasoning.

Line a 2½ pint terrine tin with cling film and spread in one third of the skate mixture. Just cover with the stock and then repeat with more skate and stock until all is used up. Press down lightly and chill for several hours or overnight until really firmly set.

Turn the terrine out onto a board, cut into thick slices and serve with a tart mayonnaise sauce.

TIPS AND VARIATIONS-

- you could instead make a sauce *gribiche* by whisking together 3 or 4 soft boiled egg yolks, a little lemon juice, dijon mustard and olive oil. Add finely chopped gherkins, capers, some of the egg white, parsley and seasoning.
- on no account let the fish overcook
- you could put the fish bones back into the court bouillon before boiling to reduce, and leave out the gelatine, as it should then, probably, set on its own
- use a very sharp and hot knife to slice the terrine

TZATZIKI

*This cucumber and yoghurt dip is a good accompaniment to curries or
other spicy dishes, as part of a mixed hors d'oeuvre or just a tasty nibble*

1 medium cucumber   NOTES
2 fat garlic cloves
250g greek yoghurt
mint and parsley
seasoning

Grate the cucumber coarsely, including the skin, and toss in a colander with a teaspoon of fine salt.
Leave it to drain for half an hour with a weighted plate on top.

Crush the garlic with a little salt in a pestle and mortar. Finely chop the mint and parsley so you have
about 2 tablespoons of each. Stir into the yoghurt with a little pepper.

Rinse the cucumber under a cold tap and squeeze it dry with your hands. Stir it into the yoghurt
mixture and chill.

TIPS AND VARIATIONS-

- avoid older cucumbers where the skin will be too coarse and seeds too large
- try with *crème fraîche*, instead of yoghurt, when the 'softening' effect with a hot
  curry will be even more noticeable
- experiment by adding finely chopped spring onion, chilli, olive oil, lime or lemon
  juice

VEGETABLE TERRINE

Time consuming but fun to make this simple terrine is a really attractive summer starter.
When cut into slices the vegetables appear as a pretty mosaic of pattern and colour

4 medium carrots

1 red pepper

3 medium courgettes

125g broad beans

250g small mushrooms

bunch of spring onions

oil and butter

400g cream cheese

3 eggs

seasoning

12 large spinach leaves

1 sachet gelatine

NOTES

Cut the carrots, pepper and courgettes, lengthwise, into thin strips and slice the mushrooms.

Bring 1½ pints lightly salted water to the boil in a large pan and cook the carrots and pepper, uncovered, until just *'al dente'*. Remove and refresh under cold water. Add the courgettes and beans to the boiling water and similarly cook. Finish with the mushrooms – which ideally will just absorb the remaining water and its flavour.

Finely chop the spring onions and simmer in a little oil and butter until soft. Put into a mixing bowl and blend in the cream cheese and the beaten eggs. Dissolve the gelatine in a ½ cup of hot water, and add it and a light seasoning to the bowl and mix to a smooth cream.

Blanch the spinach leaves for just a few seconds and drain. Use them to line the bottom and sides of a 2½ pint greased terrine dish, but reserve a few.

Pour a little of the cream cheese mixture into the bottom of the terrine – add a layer of carrots and scatter over some beans – pour in a little more of the cheese mix – add some sliced peppers and courgettes. Continue in this way, with the mushrooms in a layer of their own in the middle until all the mix and vegetables are used up, finishing with a covering of cream cheese. Press down each layer fairly firmly as you go. Cover the top with the remaining spinach leaves.

Put the terrine in a baking tin half filled with hot water and cook in a moderate oven, c.190°C, for about one hour. Allow to cool and chill in the fridge for several hours or overnight. Turn out onto a plate or board and cut into thick slices with a very sharp warmed knife.

TIPS AND VARIATIONS-
* you need roughly 1kg mixed young vegetables in all
* try with peas or french beans, but the idea is to have a mixture of colours
* take great care not to overcook the vegetables – they must be just undercooked
* the spinach lining can be horribly fiddly – using greased foil is easier but less attractive
* serve with a tomato and black olive vinaigrette and little gem lettuces

FISH

Ceviche
Couscous coated salmon
Crab cakes
Crab dumplings
Flétan au fromage
Hake fillets with thyme
Halibut with red onion orange
    and figs
Mediterranean haddock parcels
Montpellier and other savoury butters
Potted shrimps and potted crab
Salmon fish cakes
Scallops
Scallops black pudding and apple
Spicy monkfish steaks
Swordfish steaks with lime and
    coriander butter
Tuna provençale

ONE OF THE great pleasures when travelling abroad, and near the sea, is visiting the local fish markets and seeing the wonderful displays and the huge variety of freshly caught fish, crustaceans and shellfish, all colourfully arranged on their stalls. Sadly these sorts of fishermen's markets hardly seem to exist in the U.K. - nor does one find many 'wet' fishmongers to rival the magical showcases of the 'Poissonneries' of practically every provincial town in France. Amazing, really, considering our island status and extensive coastline.

However things are much better than they were, perhaps largely thanks to TV cookery programmes and celebrity chefs. Major supermarkets mostly have a good display of fresh fish, there are some wonderful fishmongers still to be found, such as in Oxford's Covered Market and there is an increasing number of 'white van' travelling fishmongers, if you choose with care. "How fresh is this fish? Fresh in this morning sir!"

There is no doubt that fish is good for you! Most fish and shellfish are low in fat and high in minerals, protein and vitamins. Very good for the cholesterol levels! But the best reason to eat fish is because, when carefully prepared and cooked it is just the most delicious of foods with such a variety of delicate flavour and textures.

As with many of the best things in life, simplicity will often give the most enjoyable results, particularly when the fish is at its freshest. Fillets or steaks of most fish, cooked, unadulterated, on a rack in a hot oven for only 6-8 minutes are very hard to beat – perhaps served with a slice of savoury butter or lemon and on a bed of chopped spinach.

CEVICHE

This is a traditional Mexican dish, but widely made in South America; the raw fish is essentially 'cooked' in the lemon (or lime) juice

2-3 mackerel fillets

medium red onion

small garlic clove

a little red chilli

juice of 2 lemons

seasoning

NOTES

Skin the fillets and cut diagonally into ½" strips. Slice the onion very thinly. Finely chop the garlic and the chilli.

Stir everything together in a shallow bowl and season lightly. Make sure the liquid covers the fish fillets; if not add more lemon juice.

Cover with foil or cling film and marinate in the fridge for an hour or two. The raw fish gradually goes opaque then a clear white colour when it is ready.

Serve on its own, or with crusty bread, as an *hors d'oeuvre*, or with a substantial salad as a light lunch dish.

TIPS AND VARIATIONS-

- you could serve this with a warm salad of sweet potatoes, slices of corn on the cob and lettuce which would be very Mexican
- lime juice is more traditional but I prefer lemon juice for this dish
- ceviche works well with many, particularly oily fish, but try it with salmon
- it is surprisingly good using scallops with finely chopped spring onion and cucumber

COUSCOUS COATED SALMON

An elegant but simple summer supper dish, easy to prepare in advance
and equally easy for a larger party

4 skinned salmon fillets

150g couscous

200ml dry white wine

saffron

1 egg

seasoning

french dressing with garlic

tomatoes

black olives

NOTES

Heat the wine gently to simmering point and whisk in 3 pinches of saffron and a little salt and pepper. Put the couscous into a shallow bowl and pour the wine over. Leave for 10 minutes or so until the liquid is absorbed then fluff it up by cutting through with a knife.

Beat the egg with a little seasoning. Coat each fillet with egg and then press into the couscous grains evenly – as though egg and breadcrumbing. Put the coated fillets onto an oven rack and bake in a medium oven, c.190°C, for 10-15 minutes until just cooked.

Meanwhile skin, deseed and chop the tomatoes and chop the olives. Stir into the french dressing. Serve the fillets individually, in a pool of vinaigrette, with french beans, new potatoes or whatever you will.

TIPS AND VARIATIONS-

- you can use a ½tsp of ground turmeric in place of the saffron
- a little finely chopped red chilli in the couscous will spice it up a bit
- the coated fillets can be covered in clingfilm and kept for some hours in the fridge until ready to cook
- decorate with chopped parsley or coriander

CRAB CAKES

Very easy to make, melt in the mouth tasty and ideal as a starter or main course.
The breadcrumbs give a much more delicate texture than fishcakes made with potato

250g fresh crab meat, white and brown

bunch of spring onions

1 tbs mayonnaise

1 tsp Dijon mustard

a handful of parsley

2-3 slices dry bread

seasoning and a few drops of tabasco

NOTES

Finely chop the spring onions and the parsley. Process the bread into crumbs.

In a large bowl mix together the crab meat, onions, mayonnaise, mustard, parsley and seasoning. Add enough breadcrumbs to create a firmly binding mixture.

By hand form the mixture into 4 or 5 patties or little flattish round cakes about ¾" thick.

Fry in oil or butter for a few minutes each side to a light golden brown. Serve at once.

TIPS AND VARIATIONS-

- double the quantities for a main course
- try for a higher proportion of white crab meat to brown
- when crumbing the bread add a little fresh ginger, garlic or chilli
- try using *crème fraîche* instead of mayonnaise
- if you need extra binding stir in an egg
- these cakes can be made well in advance and cooked at the last minute
- serve with lemon wedges, a tomato and black olive salsa or tamarind mayonnaise

For a very delicious and spicy 'Indian' crab cake, try this –

Finely chop a small onion and soften in a little hot oil; stir in a knob of ginger and two garlic cloves, both finely chopped, and cook for a few minutes. Add a tsp each of garam masala and ground coriander and cook another minute. Put into a large bowl and mix in the crabmeat, 2 tsps lemon juice, pinch of salt, some chopped coriander leaves and 1tbs mayonnaise. Then add breadcrumbs and proceed as before.

CRAB DUMPLINGS

These steamed crab dumplings make a delicious first course and can be prepared well in advance with just a few minutes steaming needed before serving

150g mixed crabmeat

2-3 spring onions

root ginger

1tsp dark soy sauce

1tsp sesame oil

½ tsp sugar

pepper

NOTES

For the dough —

3tbs plain flour

2 pinches salt

boiling water

Finely chop the spring onions. Grate the ginger - you need about one teaspoonful.

Mix these together with the crabmeat, soy sauce, oil, sugar and pepper. Leave to marinate for an hour or two.

Meanwhile make the dough. Sift the flour with the salt and add enough boiling water to form a soft dough. Knead and stir it together, dusting with flour as you go, until you have a smooth and elastic dough.

Divide the dough into 12-16 pieces rolling each into a ball. Then roll out each piece very thinly, on a lightly floured board, into a rough circle. Should be about 3" diameter.

Put a large teaspoonful of the crab mixture onto the centre of each piece. Fold them up and pinch together the edges to seal and form little parcels.

Arrange the dumplings in an oiled steamer and steam for 7-8 minutes. Serve sprinkled with soy sauce.

Tips and Variations-
* use radishes instead of spring onions
* try for at least 50% white to brown crabmeat
* try using garlic and/or spices instead of ginger
* kneading and rolling out the dough is quite tricky until you get the hang of it; you need a light touch with your fingers and plenty of flour so it does not get sticky

FLÉTAN AU FROMAGE

Halibut steaks with a cheesy topping – delicious

4 good halibut steaks
butter
seasoning
200g cheddar cheese
1tsp Dijon mustard
2tbs thick cream

Season the steaks with a little salt and plenty of pepper. Put them in a well buttered baking dish.

Grate the cheese and mix with the mustard and cream to make a thick paste. Spread it over the tops of the steaks.

Bake in a medium hot oven - c.190°C – for about 12-15 minutes until the fish is just cooked and the cheese bubbling and beginning to brown.

Serve with new potatoes and some garlicy french beans.

TIPS AND VARIATIONS-

* this is equally tasty with steaks of cod, monkfish or swordfish
* gruyère is a good alternative to cheddar
* use *crème fraîche* or yoghurt instead of cream
* I suppose this is really just a fishy welsh rarebit
* take care not to over cook – the time will depend on the thickness of the steak

HAKE FILLETS WITH THYME

*The flesh of hake – a member of the cod family - is soft but with a
delicate flavour and this simple recipe, carefully handled, brings out its best*

4-6 hake fillets

smallish red onion

2-3 cloves garlic

several thyme sprigs

1 lemon

olive oil

seasoning

NOTES

Finely chop the onion, thinly slice the garlic and coarsely grate the lemon rind. Whisk together about 2 tbs each of oil and lemon juice.

Lay the fish fillets, skin side down, on a lightly oiled roasting tin of a suitable size.

Season with salt and pepper. Sprinkle over the onion, garlic and most of the lemon zest and thyme. Drizzle over the oil and lemon juice mixture.

Put the roasting tin in a medium hot oven, about 180°C, and cook for 10-15 minutes until the fish is just done and flakes easily.

Transfer the fillets to a warm serving platter and garnish with the remaining lemon zest and thyme.

TIPS AND VARIATIONS-

- use dried thyme if fresh is not available
- cook the fillets with the skin on and skin side down
- use cod or haddock as alternatives to hake
- always be so careful not to overcook fish

HALIBUT WITH RED ONION, ORANGE AND FIGS

A surplus of figs led me to google for ideas and I came across this recipe – it is an absolute gem

4 halibut fillets

2 medium red onions

1 orange

8-10 fresh figs

handful fresh oregano

olive oil

seasoning

NOTES

Remove any skin or bone from the fillets. Cut the onions into wedges. Cut 4 or 5 long thin strips of zest from the orange and then squeeze out its juice. Halve the figs lengthwise. Finely chop the oregano.

Spread the onion wedges and orange peel in a shallow roasting tin. Sprinkle with olive oil and seasoning. Put in a medium hot oven for 15 minutes, stirring once.

Add the figs, cut side up, and half the oregano. Continue roasting for 10 minutes by when the onion should be beginning to brown at the edges. Remove.

Push everything to one side of the pan. Place the halibut fillets on the bottom and sprinkle them with the orange juice and seasoning. Partly cover with onions and figs and scatter over the remaining oregano.

Put back into a slightly hotter oven and roast for a further 10 minutes, until the fish is just cooked. Arrange on a serving dish.

TIPS AND VARIATIONS-
- the fillets should be about ¾" thick and skinless
- the figs should be ripe but firm
- you could always use dried oregano or other herbs
- always take care not to overcook fish

MEDITERRANEAN HADDOCK PARCELS

An attractive starter or main course which can be largely
prepared in advance and takes very little time anyway

500g fresh haddock fillet

8-10 thin slices prosciutto

red onion

red pepper

green or yellow pepper

10 cherry tomatoes

1tbs capers

20-30 pitted black olives

a few sprigs rosemary

olive oil

seasoning

NOTES

Deseed the peppers and chop them and the onion into a medium dice. Halve the tomatoes.

Put them all into a large shallow roasting tin together with the capers, olives and rosemary; sprinkle over with olive oil, season with sea salt and freshly ground pepper and stir around.

Put the tin into a hot oven and cook for 15-20 minutes until the vegetables are beginning to soften and are nearly cooked.

While the vegetables are cooking, cut the fish (having removed the skin and any small remaining bones) into appropriately sized largish chunks and closely wrap each piece in a slice of the prosciutto – secure with a cocktail stick if necessary.

Remove the roasting tin from the oven and reduce the heat to medium. Stir and spread the vegetables and place the haddock parcels on top. Put back in the oven and cook for 10-15 minutes until the fish is just cooked.

Serve the fish parcels on a carefully arranged bed of the vegetables.

TIPS AND VARIATIONS-

* try with other firm fleshed white fish – monkfish, cod, etc
* any smoked ham will serve well
* you can do it all in advance and leave the final cooking of the parcels until just before being ready to serve
* as always with fish take care not to overcook – it matters far less if the vegetables are overdone

MONTPELLIER AND OTHER SAVOURY BUTTERS

The recipe list looks a bit daunting but these are rather fun to make and can be very useful accompaniments to many plain grilled or baked fish and meat dishes

25g spinach

25g rocket leaves

25g parsley and chives

1 shallot and 2 cloves garlic

3 gherkins and 2tsps capers

1 raw egg yolk

2 hard boiled egg yolks

5 anchovy fillets

a little seasoning

125g unsalted butter

100ml olive oil

NOTES

Put the spinach and rocket into boiling water for just one minute. Refresh in cold water, squeeze out excess water and put into a food processor. Allow the butter to soften a little..

Roughly chop the parsley, chives, shallot, garlic and gherkins and put into the processor along with the capers, egg yolks, anchovies and softened butter.

Process it all into a *purée* and with the machine still running steadily pour in the oil. Taste for seasoning. Scrape out onto a sheet of clingfilm, form into a long roll, about 1½" diameter, and chill in the fridge until firm.   Remove the clingfilm and cut off thin slices as required.

TIPS AND VARIATIONS-

- guestimate the herb quantities – they don't need to be precise!
- if you haven't softened the butter, cut it into thick chunks first
- will keep in the fridge for a week or so, and much longer in a freezer
- you can make a simplified version using butter, a few herbs, egg yolk and anchovy. It just needs to be green and tangy
- try experimenting with different savoury butters; the following are good - with all of them it is worth adding some olive oil to the softened butter
- **Lime Butter** – add the juice and zest of two limes, chopped chives and a very little finely grated ginger
- **Beurre Maître d'Hôtel** – add 4-5 tablespoons chopped parsley and the juice of a half lemon
- **Anchovy Butter** - just add anchovies and a little garlic
- **Garlic Butter** – add lots of chopped garlic, a little shallot and use with snails and shellfish
- **Mustard Butter** – add a tablespoon of french mustard – goes well with herring and mackerel

POTTED SHRIMPS

Extremely simple to make and quite delicious - a great British classic!

250g shelled cooked brown shrimps   NOTES
125g unsalted butter
¼ tsp ground ginger
¼ tsp cayenne pepper
½ tsp grated nutmeg
4 slices bread
lemon

Melt about three quarters of the butter in a small pan over a low heat. Gently stir in the shrimps and the spices. Do not let it boil. When hot divide into four small ramekins.

Chill for half an hour or so until set. Then 'clarify' the remaining butter by heating it in the pan until foaming. Strain through a fine sieve over the potted shrimps so that each ramekin is sealed with a layer of clarified butter.

Chill in the fridge until ready to eat. Serve with 'soldiers' of warm toast and lemon wedges.

POTTED CRAB

Equally delicious

250g white crabmeat   NOTES
150g unsalted butter
walnut sized piece of root ginger
1 lime and 1 small red chilli
fresh coriander and seasoning

Grate the ginger, deseed and finely chop the chilli. Grate the zest from the lime and reserve the juice. Chop about 1 tbs of the coriander. Clarify the butter as above.

Mix everything, except the butter, together, and add a little seasoning. Put into individual ramekins. Put a coriander leaf on top of each ramekin and pour over the clarified butter.

Chill until ready to eat.

TIPS AND VARIATIONS-

- try it with prawns – its good, but not the same!
- they will keep for several days in the fridge

SALMON FISH CAKES

Traditionally fishcakes are made with mashed potatoes – this recipe, using grated raw potatoes, is interestingly different and I think much better

350g salmon fillet

250g new potatoes

1tbs capers

handful of parsley or coriander

2tbs lemon juice

seasoning

NOTES

Make sure the salmon has been skinned and boned; cut it into chunks and blend lightly in a food processor. Roughly chop the capers and herbs. Put all into a mixing bowl with the lemon juice.

Peel the potatoes and grate them coarsely, then, using both hands squeeze hard to remove as much liquid as possible. Fluff up and add to the fish in the bowl.

Add the seasoning and gently stir to combine all the ingredients. With your hands form 8-10 medium sized cakes, pressing the mixture firmly together. Fry for 5-6 minutes each side in oil and butter until golden and just cooked through.

TIPS AND VARIATIONS-

- cod or haddock or pretty well any fish can be substituted
- you may need to add an egg to help bind it all together
- you could cut the fish into very small pieces instead of blending it
- cook on a rack in a hot oven for 12-15 minutes if you prefer
- do not make the cakes too thick or the potato may not cook in the middle
- use gherkins if you have no capers
- serve with a salsa of tomato, avocado and black olives or similar

SCALLOPS

These sweet and succulent shellfish can be cooked in very many ways, and this is my favourite, but, as with most fish recipes the simplest are generally the best

8-10 scallops
olive oil
handful of parsley
2-3 cloves garlic

NOTES

This is simplicity itself but you need to be quite brave. Finely chop the parsley and garlic.

Heat the oil in a wide pan until very hot. Fry the scallops on one side until a thick gooey crust forms. Turn over and cook the other side for a few seconds only and remove to a serving dish.

Briefly sizzle the garlic and parsley, perhaps with a little more oil, and tip over the scallops.

It is the crust which brings out the flavour, so be bold and cook a little longer than you think!

SCALLOPS BLACK PUDDING AND APPLE

Much beloved, these days, by gastro pubs, this seemingly rather unlikely combination of flavours works extremely well

8 scallops
black pudding
eating apples
sunflower oil and butter

NOTES

Cut 8 thick slices of black pudding and 8 of peeled and cored apple.

Over a medium heat separately fry the apple rings until golden, the pudding until just cooked through and the scallops for about one minute each side. Pile one on top of the other and serve with a green salad.

TIPS AND VARIATIONS-
- try first coating scallops with lightly seasoned flour
- grill smaller scallops with pieces of red pepper and mushroom on a skewer
- do not slide scallops around in the pan or they will steam rather than sear

SPICY MONKFISH STEAKS

An excellent dish easily adapted for any number of people

4 monkfish steaks

1 tsp turmeric

½ tsp cayenne

2 tsp ground cumin

1 tsp salt

2 medium onions

3 cloves garlic

sunflower oil

1½ tsp mustard seeds

1½ tsp fennel seeds

400g tin of chopped tomatoes

1 tsp garam masala

handful of coriander or parsley

NOTES

Dry the steaks with kitchen paper. Mix together half each of the turmeric, cayenne, cumin and salt. Rub this mixture onto both sides of the steaks. Set aside.

Finely chop one onion and thinly slice the other. Crush and chop the garlic. Chop the coriander or parsley.

Over a highish heat put 3-4 tbs of oil in a wok or pan and when hot add the mustard and fennel seeds. After a few seconds, when they start to pop, add the onions and garlic. Stir fry for a few minutes until starting to brown. Add the remaining cumin, salt and cayenne, stir and then add the tomatoes and garam masala. Lower the heat, cover and simmer gently for 15-20 minutes.

Meanwhile, in another pan, in a little oil, quickly brown the fish steaks on both sides. Do not let them cook through.

Put the monkfish into a baking dish in a single layer. Pour over the tomato mixture and cook, uncovered, in a medium oven, for 12-15 minutes until the fish is just done.

Scatter over the chopped coriander and serve with rice or couscous and french beans.

TIPS AND VARIATIONS-

- also good with cod or tuna steaks
- if possible grind your own cumin and garam masala – see page 189
- experiment with different spices

SWORDFISH STEAKS WITH LIME AND CORIANDER BUTTER

Grilling is by far the best way to treat swordfish and it goes really well with the taste of lime in the marinade and butter

4 swordfish steaks

4tbs olive oil

juice of 1 lemon

juice of 1 lime

seasoning

125g unsalted butter

handful fresh coriander

juice and zest of a lime

NOTES

Whisk together the olive oil, lime and lemon juice with the seasoning. Pour over the swordfish steaks in a shallow dish. Chill for an hour or two in the fridge turning occasionally.

Meanwhile make the flavoured butter by first softening it. Finely chop the coriander and thoroughly mix it into the softened butter with the lime juice and zest. In greaseproof paper, the butter wrapper, form it into a neat little roll. Chill, or freeze, until firm.

Remove the fish steaks from the marinade. Cook them for three to four minutes only on each side – either under a hot grill or in a heavy ribbed grill pan.

Serve with a pat of coriander-lime butter on each steak and perhaps, new potatoes and a lightly cooked green vegetable.

TIPS AND VARIATIONS-

* substitute steaks of other white fish
* no limes – then just use lemon juice and zest, or vice versa

TUNA PROVENÇALE

A simple and easily made fish casserole with a strong Mediterranean flavour

750g thick fresh tuna steaks

8-10 very small onions

1 medium onion

500g ripe tomatoes

bay leaf and dried mixed herbs

3-4 fat cloves garlic

olive oil

seasoning

juice of ½ lemon

15-20 black olives

handful of parsley

NOTES

Peel and quarter the tomatoes. Finely chop the medium onion. Crush and chop the garlic. Chop the parsley. Cut the tuna into 2" chunks.

In a suitably sized heavy casserole dish brown the whole onions in oil for 10-12 minutes. Add the tomatoes, chopped onion, bay leaf and herbs. Simmer for 10-15 minutes.

Add the tuna chunks to the casserole with the garlic and seasoning to taste. Cover and simmer very gently 20 minutes or so until the fish is just done. Stir in the olives and lemon juice towards the end.

Serve sprinkled with parsley, and crusty french bread to mop up the juices.

TIPS AND VARIATIONS-

- pickling onions or shallots are the ones to use
- tomatoes are easily peeled by first immersing in hot water for a minute
- you could always use a tin of tomatoes
- add sliced mushrooms with the olives
- add small potatoes with the onions to make a more substantial dish
- tuna is a dense meaty fish and casseroles well but it is so important that it is only just cooked – a little too long and it is all ruined

LIGHT LUNCHES

Baked beans on toast
Catherine's courgette tart
Chicon gratin
Cucumber farcis
Eggs Florentine
Filet de porc aux moutardes
Jansson's temptation
Piperade du pays Basque
Pissaladière
Potato pie
Roasted vegetable couscous
Seafood pancakes
Spaghetti with anchovies
Courgette cakes
Tartiflette

A T ONE TIME this might have been referred to as dishes suitable for a 'ladies luncheon party' or perhaps, heavens forbid, a 'TV supper'. It is however a useful category of meal; either something pretty simple, quickly and easily prepared, or that can be made well beforehand; but whilst not insubstantial, certainly not a full or heavy meal.

Many other recipes in this book could of course be put into this category, but these few did not seem to fit in anywhere else and I felt they deserved a chapter of their own. Some are quite unusual – how many of us in the U.K. have heard of, let alone tried, Jansson's Temptation, yet it is a wonderful dish – try it!

Again the French in their wonderful brassèries are masters of this particular art and the pleasure of a simple one course meal, well presented with an attractive salad and a glass or two of wine, is very hard to beat; but we should! Originality is a considerable talent but I see no reason not to emulate and perhaps add one's own dimension to established classics.

BAKED BEANS ON TOAST

Make your own soda bread and these delicious baked beans

SODA BREAD   NOTES

    500g wholemeal flour

    1tsp salt

    1tsp bicarbonate of soda

    150ml soured cream

    2tbs milk

Grease a baking sheet with a little sunflower oil. Have ready two mixing bowls, one large one small.

In the smaller bowl, whisk together the soured cream, milk and 100ml water. Put the flour, salt and bicarbonate of soda into the larger bowl and mix well.

Stir the soured cream mixture into the flour in the larger bowl, until it amalgamates to form a dough, adding more milk or water if necessary. This is most easily done using a kitchen machine.

Knead the dough by hand to form a roughly spherical shape. Put it on the baking sheet and bake in a medium oven, c.225°C, for about 30 minutes, until cooked and nicely browning. Reserve your loaf.

BAKED BEANS   NOTES

    400g dried cannellini beans

    large onion and 3 cloves of garlic

    150g streaky bacon

    1tsp each of paprika, salt, pepper and
    mustard powder

    400g tin of chopped tomatoes

    1tsp Worcestershire sauce

    2tbs treacle

    2tsp brown sugar

Soak the beans for 6-8 hours or overnight, then rinse and drain. Chop the onion, bacon and garlic and *sauté* in a little oil in a large casserole for a few minutes until softening.

Add everything else, stir well and bring up to a simmer. Pour in enough water to cover the beans and bring back to the simmer. Cover and cook in a slow oven, c. 135°C, for three to four hours. Half way through check to ensure there is enough liquid and it is not drying out. Add more water or increase the heat as appropriate.

They will keep for several days in the 'fridge and improve still more with reheating, but try them on lightly toasted slices of your own soda bread, spread with lots of unsalted butter.

TIPS AND VARIATIONS-

•   you could add chopped black olives or sun dried tomatoes to the dough
•   you can use haricot or bartoletti beans just as well

CATHERINE'S COURGETTE TART

*This is delicious and very useful when there is a surplus of
courgettes, and, like its namesake, it looks very pretty too*

3-4 medium courgettes   NOTES
500g shortcrust pastry
2 cloves garlic
100ml olive oil
seasoning
tub of mascarpone
75g parmesan

Slice the courgettes thinly. Crush and chop the garlic. Grate the parmesan.

Mix the garlic with the oil and toss in the courgette slices with lots of seasoning. Mix half the parmesan with the mascarpone.

Roll out the pastry thinly and use it to cover a rectangular baking tray. Cut off the surplus pastry and with it form a 'lip' around the edges.

Spread the mascarpone mix evenly over the surface of the pastry, keeping within the border. Arrange the courgette slices on top in overlapping rows and sprinkle over the remaining parmesan.

Bake for 30 minutes or so in a medium hot oven, around 200°C.

Serve, hot or cold, by cutting into rectangles along the line between the courgettes, and with a little gem and tomato salad.

TIPS AND VARIATIONS-
- you could use puff pastry
- using a mandolin you can slice the courgettes in a trice
- it looks better if the courgettes are of a similar diameter

CHICON GRATIN

*This easily made Belgian dish of chicory and ham with a
cheese sauce can be prepared well in advance*

chicory heads
6-8 thin slices cooked ham

NOTES

For the Cheese Sauce;
2 medium onions
butter
flour
milk
seasoning
egg
1 tsp made mustard
150g gruyère cheese

Put the cleaned chicory heads into salted water, bring to the boil, and simmer until just tender, about 10-12 minutes. Then drain thoroughly and allow to cool.

Wrap each chicory head in a slice of ham. Arrange closely in a buttered baking dish.

Finely slice one onion and chop the other. Grate the cheese.

Prepare the cheese sauce. Soften the onions in butter in a pan, add a tablespoon or so of plain flour and stir for a few minutes. Slowly add enough milk to make a smooth and thickish sauce, stirring all the time. Add seasoning to taste, stir in the egg, mustard and then the grated cheese until melted.

Pour the sauce over the chicory, sprinkle with a little more grated cheese and bake in a medium oven, c.190°C, until just browning on top, about 20 minutes.

Tips and Variations-
• try with Worcestershire sauce instead of mustard
• use leeks instead of chicory – they need to be well cooked in advance, and to be very tender
• use part milk and part of the water that the chicory was cooked in for the sauce
• leave out the ham for a vegetable accompaniment to a roast dish or grill
• less rich if you omit the egg

CUCUMBER FARCIS

Another excellent and original way to use up surplus
cucumbers and to create an unusual light supper dish

2 cucumbers

large onion

125g rice

200g mushrooms

3 bacon rashers

2 eggs

butter

parsley and seasoning

NOTES

Cut each cucumber into 4 pieces, lengthways and across, and scrape out the seeds. Chop the onion, slice the mushrooms and cut the bacon into short strips.

Boil the cucumbers for 8-10 minutes until just soft and drain. Cook and drain the rice.

Soften the onion in a little butter, add the mushrooms and when nearly cooked add the bacon strips and stir around for a few minutes.

Meanwhile beat up the eggs with a little chopped parsley and seasoning. Make an omelette. Roll it up and slice into strips.

Add the drained rice and omelette slices to the bacon and mushroom mixture and gently turn around, briefly reheating – pile it all into the cucumber boats, sprinkle with parsley and serve very hot.

TIPS AND VARIATIONS-

- an attraction of this dish is using up bits and pieces you may have lying around eg leftover rice etc, and you can make up your own variations
- leave the cucumber unpeeled, unless the skin is coarse or you prefer without
- try with large courgettes instead of cucumbers
- there are four separate, but simple, cooking operations here – with a little thought you should be able to have them all on the go at the same time!

EGGS FLORENTINE

Everyone knows of this dish but have you ever made it, or even eaten it?

500g spinach   NOTES
4 eggs
butter
seasoning
1tbs flour
350ml milk
100g cheddar cheese
1tsp mustard powder

Wash, drain and coarsely chop the spinach. Grate the cheese.

Cook the spinach in a large pan with a knob of butter over a gentle heat, stirring occasionally, until just cooked. Season.

Meanwhile make the cheese sauce. Melt some butter in a pan over a gentle heat and stir in the flour until it forms a *roux*. Cook for a minute or two. Slowly add milk, stirring all the time, until you have a runny sauce. Add the grated cheese, mustard and seasoning. Keep stirring until the cheese has all melted and the sauce thickened.

Spread the spinach over the bottom of an ovenproof serving dish. Make four shallow depressions in the spinach and break an egg into each. Pour the cheese sauce evenly over the eggs and spinach.

Bake in a medium hot oven, c. 200°C, for about 15 minutes. The sauce should be brown and bubbling on top and the eggs just cooked through. Serve hot with slices of toast.

TIPS AND VARIATIONS-
- make the cheese sauce with some finely chopped onion

FILET DE PORC AUX MOUTARDES

This sounds too easy – but try it and you'll be hooked

1 pork tenderloin
125g button mushrooms
1 medium onion
olive oil and butter
100ml white wine
1 tsp mustard powder
1 tsp grain mustard
1tsp Dijon mustard
250g crème fraîche
seasoning

NOTES

Cut the pork fillet in half lengthways and then slice across into ¼" sections. Slice the mushrooms thinly. Halve and thinly slice the onions. Mix the mustards and *crème fraîche* together.

Gently simmer the onions in a little oil and butter until nearly soft and add the mushroom slices for a few minutes – remove and reserve.

Over a high heat stir fry the pork pieces until nearly cooked through – only 3-5 minutes. Add the onion and mushrooms, season, pour in the wine and let bubble for a few minutes.

Stir in the *crème fraîche* and mustard mixture and let it simmer a little. Relax and serve.

TIPS AND VARIATIONS-
- this is a bit like a stroganoff – serve with rice and a little gem salad
- you don't need all the mustards – any one or two will do
- take great care not to overcook the pork

JANSSON'S TEMPTATION

*This rather unusual Scandinavian gratin recipe is really very good
and even better if you can get hold of proper Swedish anchovies*

2 large onions   NOTES
5-6 medium potatoes
250g anchovies
butter and sunflower oil
2 slices dry bread
250ml single cream
200ml milk
seasoning

Halve the peeled onions and slice them very thinly. Gently soften them in a large pan, with a little oil and butter.

Meanwhile peel the potatoes. Halve lengthwise and slice thinly. Then cut crossways, so that you end up with *julienne* strips roughly 1-2 inches long. As you proceed, put into a large bowl of water, with a little lemon juice, until ready to use.

Drain the anchovies and chop into coarse chunks. Make the bread into crumbs in a food processor. Drain the potatoes. Butter a large *gratin* dish.

Spread one third of the potatoes over the bottom of the dish. Season. Scatter over a half of the anchovies and then a half of the onions. Spread over the next one third of potatoes with a little more seasoning. Then the rest of the anchovies, onions and finally potatoes on top, all in layers. Press gently down, by hand, to firm it all up.

Mix the cream and milk and bring up to a simmer. Pour enough over the *gratin* so that the potatoes are visible but not smothered. Spread the breadcrumbs over the top and dot with butter. Bake for 50-60 minutes in a medium hot oven.

TIPS AND VARIATIONS-
* use fresh anchovies preserved in oil rather than the tinned sort
* Swedish anchovies preserved in spiced brine are traditionally correct
* very good with rather larger amounts of sweet cured herring fillet, or even smoked salmon; in fact any preserved oily fish will work
* the potatoes really need to be pretty skinny or they will not cook through
* use the onions raw for a stronger oniony flavour
* for a lighter version omit the cream – try using beer
* reheats well and its not bad cold

PIPERADE DU PAYS BASQUE
A good dish for a serious breakfast or light lunch

500g ripe tomatoes
5-6 eggs
medium onion
clove garlic
2 green peppers
4-5 bacon slices
3tbs olive oil
seasoning

NOTES

Skin and roughly chop the tomatoes, deseed and slice the peppers, finely chop the onion and crush the garlic.

In a frying pan or wok very gently cook the onion, pepper and garlic for about 15 minutes until softened. Add the tomatoes and seasoning and continue cooking and stirring for a few minutes until most of the liquid has evaporated.

Meanwhile fry or grill the bacon rashers separately.

Beat the eggs and add to the vegetable mixture and stir around until the eggs are lightly scrambled. Serve in a shallow dish with the bacon rashers on top.

Tips and Variations-
- gammon rashers make a more substantial dish
- the garlic is optional for breakfast
- tinned tomatoes will do though not so good
- use red peppers instead of green or as well as
- take great care not to overcook

PISSALADIÈRE

*This is a Provençale pie made with onions, tomatoes and anchovies
and is easily prepared well in advance.*

500g short crust flan pastry   NOTES

600g onions

3 large cloves garlic

3-4 large tomatoes

can of anchovy fillets

black olives, pitted

olive oil and seasoning

Roll out the pastry and line a greased 10" circular flan or pie tin. Prick the pastry, line it with greaseproof paper and weight it with baking beans. Blind bake in a medium hot oven; c.200°C – for 15 minutes. Remove and allow to cool.

Meanwhile slice the onions very thinly. Crush and chop the garlic. Skin and slice the tomatoes. Halve the olives and cut the anchovies in half lengthwise.

Cook the onions in 3tbs olive oil very gently in a large pan, covered, stirring from time to time, until soft – about 20 minutes.

Add the tomatoes, garlic and seasoning. Cook for 5-10 minutes, uncovered, over a slightly raised heat, stirring regularly, until any liquid has evaporated and the mixture is fairly stiff.

Spread this mixture evenly over the pastry in the flan tin. Arrange the anchovy slivers over the surface in a criss cross pattern and fill the spaces with the olive halves.

Sprinkle over a little olive oil and bake in the medium hot oven for 20-25 minutes.

Tips and Variations-

- use a flan tin with a removable bottom
- skin tomatoes by covering with boiling water; leave for 40 seconds; the skin then slips off
- if you make your own pastry, make it fairly rich
- use good quality olives
- the pie can be made well in advance and then put in the oven when you are ready

POTATO PIE

A firm and favourite family dish, either hot or cold and almost better reheated

250g gammon or bacon
250g onions
250g cheddar cheese
750g potatoes
6 eggs
250ml milk
3-4 cloves garlic
4tbs chopped fresh herbs
oil and butter
seasoning

NOTES

Coarsely dice the gammon, chop the onions and gently fry both in a little oil and butter for a few minutes until the onions are soft.

Grate the raw potatoes and squeeze the liquid out of them, a handful at a time. Grate the cheese and crush the garlic with a little salt.

Break the eggs into a large mixing bowl and stir in the milk, cheese and garlic with plenty of fresh ground black pepper and the herbs. Mix well.

Fold in the grated potatoes together with the onion and gammon mixture. Check seasoning.

Grease an appropriately sized warmed shallow baking dish and fill with the potato pie mixture – put in a medium oven – 190°C – and bake for 40-50 minutes when the top should be nicely browned and the potatoes tender.

TIPS AND VARIATIONS-

- use more or less garlic depending on your taste
- add some emmental to the cheese and sprinkle a little on top
- parsley, tarragon, chives, oregano are best but dried mixed herbs can substitute
- add mushrooms or courgettes for more interest
- the secret of this dish is grating the raw potatoes. Squeezing the water out is rather messy but necessary and well worth the effort

ROASTED VEGETABLE COUSCOUS

*One of those great dishes where one can use up whatever left over
vegetables are lying around or are available in the garden.*

250g couscous

olive oil

4 fat garlic cloves

seasoning

300ml chicken stock

AROUND 1KG OF 4 OR 5 OF THE FOLLOWING

red or yellow peppers

red onions

leeks

mushrooms

parsnips

carrots

french beans

aubergine

courgettes

etc etc

Clean and prepare your chosen vegetables and cut them all into ½" chunks.

Bring the stock to the boil and pour over the couscous in a shallow bowl and keep warm for 10 minutes. Use a knife to separate the grains and fluff it up.

Put all the vegetables into a large baking tray with the unpeeled garlic cloves. Mix in the olive oil and seasoning. Put in a hot oven, c. 225°C, for 40-50 minutes, stirring from time to time, until cooked and browned on the edges.

Squeeze the pulp from the garlic cloves and mix all together with the vegetables and couscous.

Serve decorated with any chopped green herbs.

TIPS AND VARIATIONS-
- this is equally good hot, cold or tepid!
- garlic cooked like this in the skin loses all of it's pungency and is wonderfully aromatic

SEAFOOD PANCAKES

Stuffed pancakes can create a whole range of really tasty, attractive and original dishes which can be prepared well in advance. Seafood stuffing is one of the best

FOR THE PANCAKES

125g plain flour

pinch of salt

1 egg and 1 egg yolk

200ml milk

100ml water

1tbs melted butter

FOR THE FILLING

200g smoked haddock

200g fresh haddock

100g prawns, cooked and peeled

40g butter

1tbs plain flour

400ml milk

nutmeg and seasoning

gruyère cheese

NOTES

Make the pancake batter by whisking together all the ingredients, keeping the melted butter until last, until it is smooth with the consistency of thin cream.

Make 12 to 14 pancakes in the usual way. Stack them up and reserve.

Gently poach the smoked and fresh haddock in the milk for a few minutes until barely cooked. Reserve the milk. Let cool a little, remove the skin and any bones, and coarsely flake the fish.

Make a white *béchamel* sauce with the butter, flour and enough of the reserved milk to make it thick and creamy. Add seasoning and grated nutmeg. Fold the fish and prawns into the sauce.

Divide the filling up between the pancakes and fold over the sides, so that the filling is completely enclosed. Put the stuffed pancakes on a large buttered dish, brush the tops with melted butter, sprinkle some grated gruyère over the tops, and bake in a medium hot oven for 15 minutes.

Serve with a few lightly dressed salad leaves.

TIPS AND VARIATIONS-

- pancakes can be made well in advance and will keep in the fridge for a day or two
- you can cook the pancakes for slightly longer on one side and not cook the other side
- take great care not to overcook – they need to be soft enough to fold
- most other fish can be used but try to get a contrast of taste and colour
- you can stuff pancakes with pretty well anything, useful for leftovers, but you will always need a binding sauce

SPAGHETTI WITH ANCHOVIES

A rich and filling dish that can be prepared in minutes

400g spaghetti

butter

2 tins of anchovies

200ml crème fraîche

seasoning

parsley

NOTES

Boil the spaghetti in plenty of salted water, with a little olive oil, until cooked *al dente.*

Separately melt a knob of butter in a pan and add the anchovy fillets, with oil from the tin, and crush with a wooden spoon until they dissolve. Add the *crème fraîche* and stir to a smooth paste, season, and let bubble for a minute or two until reduced to a rich coating sauce.

Toss briefly together with the well drained spaghetti and chopped parsley.

VARIATIONS AND TIPS-
* you can of course do this with any pasta; fettuccini or tagliatelli are very good
* anchovy essence can be added to strengthen, or more *crème fraîche* to weaken the flavour

COURGETTE CAKES

These tasty vegetarian burgers are an excellent way to use up surplus courgettes

3 medium courgettes

1 medium shallot

knob of ginger and ½ a red chilli

2tsps wholegrain mustard

1 egg and 2 slices dry bread

handful of fresh coriander leaves

NOTES

Grate the courgettes and by hand squeeze them to remove as much liquid as possible – the drier the better. Finely chop the shallot and chilli. Process the bread into crumbs. Beat the egg. Chop the coriander.

Mix everything together in a large bowl, adding enough crumbs to make a firm mixture. Season to taste.

Form the mixture into thickish burger shaped patties. Fry gently in oil and butter for 8-10 minutes each side, until golden and just cooked through.

TIPS AND VARIATIONS-
* if the courgettes are larger, quarter lengthwise and remove the pith

TARTIFLETTE

A 'traditional' dish from Savoie in the French Alps

1kg potatoes
2 medium onions
250g smoked bacon
400g emmental cheese
olive oil
1tsp dried thyme
400ml milk
300ml crème fraîche
seasoning

Halve and thinly slice the onions. Peel and slice the potatoes ¼" thick. Dice the bacon fairly small. Mix the milk and *crème fraîche* together. Slice the cheese fairly thinly.

Generously season and gently cook the potatoes in the milky mixture in a wide pan, covered, until only just *al dente.* Stir occasionally so they do not stick together. About 15 minutes or so. Drain the potatoes but save the milk mixture.

In another pan, in a little oil, fry the onion slices with the bacon bits for 10-15 minutes until the onion is softened and the bacon crisping. Add the thyme half way through.

In a suitably sized shallow baking dish make layers of potato, onion and bacon, and cheese, finishing with a cheese layer. Dribble in the milk as you go so that the cheese is just not covered.

Bake in a medium hot oven, c.180-200°C, for 15-20 minutes until the cheese is bubbling and browning. Serve with a green salad.

TIPS AND VARIATIONS-

- this 'traditional' recipe was invented in the 1980's by reblochon to promote their cheese – it is actually much better made with emmental
- use a waxy potato such as *desirée*
- you could add a layer of thinly sliced mushrooms
- everything can be prepared well in advance of the final baking

CHICKEN

HENRY IV (OF France) once famously said that he wanted no peasant in his land to be so poor that he could not afford to have a chicken in his pot, every Sunday. No doubt Henry had in mind a farm fresh, free range and organic chicken, although probably not British! Today, whilst a factory chicken can be the cheapest of meats, quality is again increasingly appreciated and I suspect those French peasants did not realise how fortunate they were.

I gave chicken a chapter on its own because of its great versatility; and the extraordinarily wide range of recipes available. It can be combined so well with such a huge variety of ingredients. Free range chickens are now so widely available it really does pay to use them whenever possible – the taste is infinitely superior. Do remember that 'organic' is not the same as 'free range', nor indeed vice versa. When delicately cooked chicken can be the most subtle of flavours.

Always take care not to overcook chicken; it is best when still a little moist. When browning chicken pieces that may be a bit soggy, a coating of seasoned flour works wonders, and it helps to thicken any sauce in which it is cooked. The best way to do this is to put the seasoned flour in a plastic bag with the chicken and shake around for a few moments – not a bag with holes in!

A whole chicken can easily be cut into eight pieces – thighs and drumsticks, wings with a little breast attached and two breasts – the carcase can then be made into stock.

Chicken recipes appear, in different guises, in several other chapters of this book; but, for a Sunday lunch, a whole roast chicken, perfectly cooked, crisp and moist, is very hard to beat.

CARIBBEAN CHICKEN
AND BLACK BEANS

*aka Chicken Mojo con Frijoles Negros and apparently very
authentic this dish works well and has been a great success*

3-4 chicken breasts

3 tsps ground cumin

6-7 fat garlic cloves

small red chilli

olive oil

seasoning

juice of one lime and one orange

100g dried black beans

2 medium onions

1 green and 2 red peppers

handful oregano, coriander or parsley

glass dry white wine

glass dry martini

NOTES

Soak the beans overnight in cold water. Drain and rinse, then simmer in fresh, slightly salted, water until soft, 10-20 minutes. Drain and reserve.

Deseed the chilli and crush it, with 3 of the garlic cloves, 1 tsp of the cumin and a pinch of salt, in a pestle and mortar, to a coarse paste. Heat a little oil in a small pan and blend in the paste. Let it simmer for a few minutes – remove, cool and stir in the lime and orange juice.

Pour this mixture over the chicken pieces in a shallow bowl, turning it around so all the pieces are well covered and marinate in the fridge for 2-3 hours.

Meanwhile, chop coarsely the onions, oregano and peppers; crush and chop the remaining 4 garlic cloves, and gently simmer it all with the remaining cumin in a little oil until just soft, about 10-15 minutes.

Turn up the heat, season and tip in the wine and martini. Boil and stir around until the liquid has just evaporated. Stir in the reserved black beans and simmer very gently for 20-30 minutes.

Remove the chicken pieces from the marinade and fry briskly in a little oil for a few minutes each side until lightly browned. Pour over any remaining marinade juices, cover, and cook slowly for 15-20 minutes until the chicken is just cooked through.

Cut the chicken pieces into thick slices and serve on a bed of the black bean mixture.

TIPS AND VARIATIONS-
* serve with rice or couscous and a green salad
* use skin on free range chicken scored with a sharp knife to help absorb the marinade
* 100g of dried beans when soaked absorb water to become 400g
* use tinned beans to speed things up

CHICKEN WITH LETTUCE
AND PETIT POIS

This is a very french dish with a wonderful combination of flavours

one free range chicken

olive oil and butter

2 shallots or a medium onion

10-12 cloves garlic

handful of fresh green herbs

bay leaf

seasoning

glass of white wine

2 bunches of spring onions

400g frozen petit pois

2 little gem lettuces

150ml chicken stock

NOTES

Cut the chicken into 8 pieces, and save the drumsticks for another day. Put the carcase into a large pan of water and simmer for an hour or two to make some stock.

Finely chop the shallots or onion. Peel the garlic cloves and cut off the spring onion heads. Shred the lettuce.

Season the chicken pieces well and brown quickly in oil, in an ovenproof pan. Add a little butter, the chopped shallots, herbs and cloves of garlic whole. Cover and put in a medium oven, c.200°C, for 15-20 minutes until just cooked.

Meanwhile, in another pan, gently fry the whole spring onions in a little butter, add the bay leaf and about 150ml of stock. Stir in the peas, season to taste and simmer very gently for 5 minutes or so until the peas are nearly cooked. Fold in the shredded lettuce and stir for a few moments until it has wilted.

Take the chicken, garlic etc from the pan and keep warm. Skim off excess fat from the pan; add the wine and boil to reduce by half.

Arrange the lettuce, little onions and peas on a hot serving dish; put the chicken and garlic on top and pour over the reduced winey juices.

TIPS AND VARIATIONS-
- do not worry about using so much garlic; it becomes mild and delicate when cooked this way
- use a stock cube and chicken portions if you wish

CHICKEN WITH CUCUMBER

*The cucumber gives this unusual dish a light fresh taste
which contrasts well with the chicken and the creamy sauce*

3-4 chicken breasts   NOTES
seasoned flour
oil and butter
2 medium onions
2 cucumbers
250ml crème fraîche
seasoning

Cut each chicken breast into 3 pieces and coat in the seasoned flour. Finely chop the onions. Quarter the cucumbers lengthways, slice out the seeds and chop into larger chunks, leaving the skin on.

Brown the chicken pieces quickly for a few minutes in a little oil and butter. Add the onion and simmer for a few minutes until the onion softens..

Add the cucumber chunks, *crème fraîche* and seasoning. Cover and simmer very gently for 30 minutes or so, turning occasionally, until the chicken is just cooked.

The sauce should now be a thick coating consistency – if not either add a little *beurre manié*, or remove the chicken and cucumber and reduce.

Serve with new potatoes and a green salad.

Variations and Tips-

- free range chicken is, as always, infinitely superior
- the easiest way to coat the chicken pieces is to put them into a plastic bag with the flour and seasoning and give it a good shake
- skin the cucumber if preferred or if it is coarse or old
- use greek yoghurt or thick cream instead of *crème fraîche*
- the cucumber pieces need to retain a little 'crunch' and not go mushy

COQ AU VIN

There are many variations of this celebrated dish, but this is as good as any, and is not difficult, although it can become quite sophisticated with care and attention

1 medium chicken

seasoned flour

200g thick bacon chunks

12 whole button onions

1tbs olive oil and 50g butter

3-4 cloves garlic, crushed

bouquet of bay leaf, thyme and parsley

2tbs brandy

½ bottle red wine

½ pint chicken stock

200g button mushrooms

seasoning

NOTES

Joint the chicken into eight pieces and shake in a plastic bag with the flour to coat evenly.

Using a wide pan on a high heat, quickly brown the chicken pieces, onions and bacon chunks in the oil and butter and remove to a large casserole – probably in two or three batches.

Add the garlic, herbs and seasoning to the casserole and cook over slow heat for 5-10 minutes. Add the heated brandy and ignite. Shake gently until the flames die down.

Then add the wine, stock and mushrooms, cover, and simmer very gently for 30-40 minutes until the chicken is just cooked.

Remove all the pieces to a serving dish; reduce the sauce to a light coating consistency, or thicken with a *beurre manié* and pour over the chicken. Decorate with chopped parsley.

TIPS AND VARIATIONS-

- stock made from the chicken carcase is best, but a cube will do
- most importantly do not overcook the chicken
- drink a wine similar to that used in the cooking; the dish can take it's name from the wine used in the cooking eg coq au chambertin, coq au reisling etc
- try making it with white wine – good and interestingly different
- serve with new potatoes tossed in butter and parsley

JELLY'S STUFFED CHICKEN THIGHS

A good dish for a casual supper party which can largely be prepared in advance.
Served with a tomato and red onion salsa it is quite delicious

4 large chicken thighs, skin on

medium onion

3 bacon rashers

2 medium mushrooms

seasoning

handful of parsley

3 slices dry bread

medium red chilli, deseeded

1 large beaten egg

NOTES

Remove the bone from the thighs and roll out the chicken flesh, skin side down.

Finely chop the onion, bacon and mushrooms. Stir fry them in a little butter for 5-6 minutes until the onion has softened. Season well.

Let the mixture cool and then spread it evenly over the thighs. Roll up each thigh so the mixture is contained and secure with two cocktail sticks, forming a neat little parcel.

Coarsely chop the chilli, parsley and bread. Put in a blender and process into crumbs. Roll the thighs in the beaten egg and press into the breadcrumb mixture, coating evenly.

Cook, on a rack, in a medium hot oven for 25-30 minutes until lightly browned and the chicken just cooked through. Serve with french beans, potato mash and this salsa -

The Salsa - mix well together:- half a finely chopped red onion; the flesh of 4 large tomatoes, skinned, deseeded and roughly chopped; 1tsp grain mustard; juice of a lemon; large garlic clove crushed with salt; 4tbs olive oil; pepper to taste.

TIPS AND VARIATIONS-

* this is a good easy dish for a large number as you are really only limited by the size of the oven rack - but do leave space between each thigh
* invent other stuffings, eg. apple and apricot, etc

LEBANESE LEMON CHICKEN
an elegant and easily made family dish

1 free range chicken
olive oil
2 cloves garlic
1 lemon
bunch of spring onions
handful of mixed fresh herbs
seasoning

NOTES

Joint the chicken into 8 pieces. Finely chop the onions and garlic. Chop the herbs. Grate the rind from the lemon and squeeze out the juice.

In a shallow serving dish mix together 4-5tbs oil with the onion, garlic, herbs, lemon rind and juice and seasoning. Put in the chicken pieces and turn around so that they are well coated in the marinade.

Cover with foil and marinate in the fridge for several hours, or until you are ready to cook.

Remove the chicken from the marinade and brown in a hot pan for a few minutes each side.

Put the chicken back into the shallow serving dish, sprinkle over a little more salt and pepper and stir around in the marinade. Bake, uncovered, for about 30 minutes in a medium oven, c.180°C, until the chicken is just cooked through.

TIPS AND VARIATIONS-

- serve on a bed of lentils with couscous, or rice and a green salad
- you could add some grated ginger to the marinade
- use chicken portions; or just breasts which you can thickly slice to serve
- use the chicken carcase to make stock
- if you make small slashes into the chicken it helps to absorb the marinade
- parsley, thyme, tarragon, oregano, marjoram, chives or coriander will do; whatever herbs are available

LEEK, LEMON AND CHICKEN COUSCOUS

*A wonderfully aromatic dish that is equally good hot or cold
and can be made ready for the table well in advance*

3-4 medium leeks

2-3 skinless chicken breasts

2-3 cloves garlic

100g watercress

1 lemon

olive oil

180g couscous

350ml chicken stock

2tbs blanched almonds

NOTES

Cut the leeks into 3" lengths and slice lengthwise. Cut the chicken into 'nugget' sized strips. Thinly pare the zest from the lemon and cut into small pieces.

Put the leeks into boiling salted water and blanch for 4-5 minutes until just done. Drain and reserve.

Put the chicken pieces in a bowl with the juice of half the lemon and 1tbs of oil; mix well and set aside to marinate for an hour. Put the watercress, lemon zest and garlic into a food processor and finely chop.

Bring the stock up to simmering point. Pour into a large serving bowl, add 1tbs of oil and the remaining lemon juice. Stir in the couscous, cover with a cloth and leave for 10 minutes or so until the liquid has all been absorbed. Fluff it up with a fork.

Meanwhile, over a highish heat, fry the almonds in a little oil until going golden; remove and reserve. Add some more oil and quickly stir fry the chicken pieces.

Stir the watercress mixture into the couscous followed by the almonds, the chicken and the leeks. Season to taste. Sprinkle over a little olive oil and any remaining lemon juice. Warm in a medium oven until ready to serve.

TIPS AND VARIATIONS-

- will keep in the fridge for several days, but serve at room temperature
- you could use pine nuts instead of almonds
- if you put the leeks into a larger quantity of boiling water , they will come back to the boil very quickly – a useful tip if blanching anything for just a few minutes
- there are quite a number of different operations involved in this recipe and you can have fun working out the most efficient way to proceed!
- the garlic is uncooked so will be quite strong – use less if you wish

POULET NORMANDE

*It's a bit tedious pushing the sauce through a sieve but well
worth the effort for the lovely smooth appley taste*

1 medium chicken

150g thick bacon
1 medium onion
500g apples
2tbs flour
oil and butter
175ml each cider and chicken stock
seasoning
4tbs crème fraîche

Joint the chicken into 8 pieces, but save the drumsticks for another day. Coat with flour by shaking in a plastic bag with seasoning. Cut the bacon into coarse chunks. Finely chop the onion. Peel and core the apples and roughly chop.

In a wide pan, or wok, brown the chicken in oil and butter for a few minutes along, with the bacon bits; remove and keep warm.

Gently fry the onion and apple until softening; stir in any remaining flour and cook for a few minutes. Stir in the stock and cider and bring up to the boil.

Return the chicken and bacon to the pan, cover and simmer very gently for about 30-40 minutes, until the chicken is just cooked.

Dish the chicken and bacon bits and keep warm. Press the sauce through a sieve and, if necessary, reduce to a coating consistency. Check seasoning. Pour over the chicken and swirl around the *crème fraîche.*

TIPS AND VARIATIONS-

- garnish with triangles of fried bread, fried apple rings and chopped parsley
- you can just liquidise the sauce, but it will be a bit fibrous and is not the same as when pushed through a sieve
- stock cubes are an adequate substitute for the real thing

POULET SAUTÉ AU VINAIGRE

If you use a free range chicken you can always taste the difference!

1 medium chicken
1tbs seasoned flour
250 ml red wine vinegar
250ml chicken stock
12-15 shallots
6-8 cloves garlic
2tbs olive oil and 50g butter
handful of tarragon leaves
seasoning

NOTES

Joint the chicken into 8 pieces and lightly dust with seasoned flour. Peel the shallots and garlic cloves and chop 3 tbs of tarragon leaves.

In a large pan over a highish heat cook the chicken pieces in oil and butter for 8-10 minutes until nicely browned all over. Remove and set aside on a plate.

Briefly brown the shallots and garlic, whole, in the remaining oil and butter.

Lower the heat. Return the chicken pieces to the pan, pour over the stock and vinegar and scatter over the tarragon. Simmer very gently, without covering, for 40-50 minutes until just cooked. Turn the chicken half way through so their other sides cook in the sauce.

Remove the chicken, shallots and garlic and arrange on a serving dish. The remaining sauce should now be well concentrated. Whisk in a little butter, pour over the chicken and scatter with any remaining tarragon sprigs.

TIPS AND VARIATIONS-
- if you start well in advance you can make a stock with the chicken carcase
- the trick is to ensure both chicken and shallots are just cooked - so prod occasionally with a sharp knife to check
- the garlic cloves become very mild when cooked whole
- this goes well with new potatoes and french beans or peas
- when finishing add a tbs of *crème fraîche*, instead of butter, to soften the vinegar

POULET SAUTÉ AU VIN BLANC

An elegant but very simple dish which is a speciality of the various regions of France famous for white wine. It takes its name from the variety of wine used – eg. poulet sauté au chablis, poulet sauté au muscadet or poulet sauté au champagne etc

1 free range chicken

NOTES

butter

olive oil

seasoning

1 medium onion

200g button mushrooms

2 glasses dry white wine

200ml double cream

Joint the chicken into eight pieces and dry them. Finely chop the onion and thinly slice the mushrooms.

In a wide pan, *sauté* the chicken pieces briskly in a little oil and butter for a few minutes until nicely browned. Season, cover, and cook over a very low heat for 30 minutes or so until just done.

Remove the chicken and keep warm. Add onion and mushrooms to the pan and stir for one minute over a highish heat; then add the wine and boil rapidly until reduced by a half.

Stir in the cream, replace the chicken pieces and simmer very gently for a few minutes until the sauce thickens slightly. Decorate with any chopped green herbs.

TIPS AND VARIATIONS-
- you can of course use chicken portions
- *crème fraîche* or yoghurt will make it less rich
- good served with rice or couscous and a green salad
- a similar wine should be drunk with the dish

TARRAGON CHICKEN

A delicate and subtle tasting dish when made with a decent free range chicken –
quick and easy to make when there is plenty of tarragon in the garden

4 chicken breasts

60g butter

large bunch of tarragon

250ml double cream

seasoning

lemon juice

Cut chicken breasts into ¾" wide pieces. Strip the tarragon leaves from their stalks.

Melt the butter in a wide pan, or wok, over a medium heat and when sizzling stir in the chicken pieces and tarragon. Stir fry for a few minutes until nicely coloured.

Add the cream and simmer a few moments. Add seasoning and lemon juice to taste and simmer a few minutes when the chicken should be just done.

TIPS AND VARIATIONS-

* use skin on breasts which helps keep the flesh moist and adds to the flavour
* use yoghurt or *crème fraîche* to make it less rich
* serve on a bed of rice or couscous with a little gem salad

TROPICAL CHICKEN

A delightfully fresh tasting dish with an exotic aura

6-8 skinless chicken portions

2 medium onions

½ a fresh pineapple

2 corn on the cobs

a large red pepper

2 limes

250g crème fraîche

butter and olive oil

seasoning

½ bottle sweet white wine

handful of fresh herbs

Put a little oil and butter into a heavy pan and *sauté* the chicken pieces for a few minutes until lightly browned all over. Season. Remove and set on one side.

Meanwhile thinly slice both onions. Peel and cut the pineapple into bite size pieces. Cook the cobs in boiling water and slice off the corns. Slice the pepper. Thinly pare the rind from one lime and squeeze out the juice. Cut the other into segments. Chop the herbs.

Put the onion into any remaining fat in the pan and fry gently for a few minutes until softening. Add the chicken pieces, the pineapple, pepper, wine, lime juice and rind. Mix it all together. Cover and simmer for 20 minutes or so, until the chicken is just cooked.

Remove the chicken and all the bits and keep warm. Boil the remaining liquid until well reduced. Lower the heat, stir in the *crème fraîche* and corn and warm through, but do not let it boil. Stir in half the chopped herbs.

Return the chicken to the pan and mix all together. Arrange on a serving dish, scatter over the remaining herbs and garnish with the lime segments.

Tips and Variations-

* serve with rice or couscous and a crisp green salad
* use greek style or low fat yoghurt instead of *crème fraîche*
* the sauce should be of a coating consistency; not too thick, nor too thin
* you could use a lemon instead of the limes
* use tinned pineapple and sweetcorn
* use mango instead of the corn

SOME MEAT

Braised belly pork
Braised lamb shanks
Duck legs in orange sauce
Épigrammes d'agneau
Grilled duck breasts
Pork schnitzel
Shepherd's pie
Spicy leg of lamb
Steak and kidney pudding
Stuffed cabbage
Twice cooked leg of lamb and mash
Whitsun lamb

ROASTS, GRILLED CHOPS, steaks or cutlets are all pretty standard fare and simple enough ways of cooking meat. Many other recipes in this book involve meat, but these rich and substantial dishes all involve a fair degree of preparation, and will reward the effort; most might make a good alternative for a Sunday lunch or a centrepiece for a serious supper party.

They are all very traditional dishes in their way and perhaps rather against the trend of modern cuisine, which is a good enough reason to give them a go! but most importantly they do just taste so very good.

For example, the pork schnitzel is a dish I often make; unlike the others it is relatively quick and easy, yet I have never come across it anywhere else.

BRAISED BELLY PORK

*This wonderfully tasty dish can largely be made a day in
advance and then pan fried at the last moment*

2kg piece of belly pork   NOTES
pepper
thyme or marjoram
grated rind of a lemon
olive oil
2 celery stalks
1 leek
medium onion
3 garlic cloves
3 bay leaves
3tbs soy sauce
large glass of medium sherry

Remove the rind and bones from the pork. Lay it fatty side down and sprinkle over the pepper, lemon zest and thyme. Roll it up and tie securely with string.

Slice the leek and coarsely chop the celery, onion and garlic.

Brown the meat all over in a little oil. Remove, and in the same oil, cook the celery, leek, onion and garlic for a minute or two. Put the meat in a suitably sized casserole and surround with the vegetables. Add the bay leaves and pour over the soy sauce and sherry and water to half way up.

Cover the casserole, bring to the boil and then simmer in a slow oven, c.140°C, for 3-4 hours, by when the meat should be very tender.

Remove the meat and allow to cool. Keep in the fridge until required.

Strain the cooking juices and discard the vegetables. Cool and skim off all the fat. Put the juices in a small pan and boil hard until reduced by about half to a sauce like consistency.

When you are ready to eat, cut the pork into thick slices and pan fry over a highish heat for 2-3 minutes each side and serve with the warmed sauce.

TIPS AND VARIATIONS –

- free range pork, Gloucestershire Old Spot for example, is greatly superior
- another way to serve the braised pork would be to carve it from the joint with the cooked vegetables, perhaps having put in more of them
- vary the braising ingredients with, say, ginger slices, whole garlic cloves, balsamic vinegar or red current jelly – experiment
- save the rind and roast it for pork crackling

BRAISED LAMB SHANKS

*Lamb shanks are cheap and this spicy and very tasty dish reheats well.
The anchovies really intensify the flavour.*

4 lamb shanks   NOTES
sea salt and peppercorns
2tsp coriander seeds
small dried red chilli
sprig fresh rosemary
1tsp dried marjoram
1tbs flour

2tbs olive oil
4 garlic cloves
2 medium carrots
celery head
3 medium onions
2tbs balsamic vinegar
large glass of dry white wine
tin anchovy fillets
tin plum tomatoes

Put the salt, peppercorns, coriander, chilli, rosemary and marjoram through a spice grinder. Mix with the flour and toss it all together with the shanks in a plastic bag until the lamb is well coated.

In a wide pan or wok brown the lamb shanks in the olive oil and then remove to a casserole.

Coarsely slice the garlic, carrots, celery and onions. Gently soften them all in the remaining olive oil. Add the balsamic vinegar and let it all reduce to a syrupy consistency. Add the wine and simmer for a few minutes, then add the anchovies (without the oil from the tin).

Pour the vegetable mixture over the lamb in the casserole and add the tomatoes whole, but not the juice. Bring to the boil, cover and simmer in a slow oven, abt 140-150°C, for 1½ hours or so.

Remove the lid and cook for another 30-40 minutes, when the meat should be almost falling from the bone. Serve decorated with chopped herbs.

TIPS AND VARIATIONS-

- a small coffee grinder is the most useful means of grinding your own spices.
- the meat should be just falling from the bone- if not cook a little longer
- as with most casseroles it will actually improve with reheating and so can be prepared a day in advance –thus why it is such a popular pub dish
- you can vary the herbs and spices to your hearts content

DUCK LEGS IN AN ORANGE SAUCE

This simple method gives succulent meat with a good crispy skin

4 duck legs

2 oranges

seasoning

medium onion

1tbs flour

1dsp red currant jelly

glass of port

watercress

NOTES

Line a roasting tin with kitchen foil. Thickly slice one of the oranges and spread over the foil. Put the duck joints on top of the orange slices and season with salt and pepper.

Put in a very hot oven, c.250°C, for 20-25 minutes to brown on top, then remove.

Cover the pan with kitchen foil and put in a very slow oven, c.125°C, for 1-1½ hours until the duck is tender.

Strain off all the fat and liquid from the pan, and reserve, and put the pan back into a very hot oven, uncovered, for just a few minutes to crisp the duck.

Meanwhile make the sauce. Chop the onion and gently cook in 2 tbs of the reserved duck fat for a few minutes until softened. Stir in the flour. Add sufficient water (or stock) to make thinnish sauce. Simmer gently and stir in the jelly, the port and a little seasoning.

Pour the sauce around the duck legs and serve garnished with watercress and orange slices.

TIPS AND VARIATIONS-

- use both thigh and drumstick
- this recipe is ideally cooked in an Aga
- prick the skin of the duck to help release fat when cooking

ÉPIGRAMMES D'AGNEAU

Breast of lamb is something that tends to get left in the freezer
This is a classic french dish making good use of a cheap cut of meat

1kg lamb breast
medium onion
medium carrot
stick of celery
bay leaf, parsley and thyme
salt and pepper

seasoned flour
1 egg
breadcrumbs
oil and butter

500g peas
lemon

NOTES

Slice the onion, carrot and celery. Beat the egg. Make the breadcrumbs. Season the flour.

Put the meat into a large enough pan with the vegetables, herbs and seasoning. Add water to just cover; cover the pan and simmer very gently until the lamb is just tender, about 1-1½ hours.

Drain the meat. Remove the bones and as much of the fat as possible. Lay out flat with a weighted board on top and cool.

Cut into 1" wide fingers, then coat with the seasoned flour, beaten egg and breadcrumbs.

Fry quickly in hot oil and butter until golden on both sides. and drain on absorbent paper.

Meanwhile cook the peas. *Purée* in a blender, or push through a sieve, and stir in a pat of butter.

Serve with the lamb fingers arranged around a mound of *puréed* peas with slices of lemon.

TIPS AND VARIATIONS-
- the lamb breast may be in one or more pieces
- removing the fat is a messy but, necessary, job
- you could use best end of neck which would be much less fatty
- scatter some finely chopped mint over the finished dish
- instead of lemon serve with a piquant sauce, such as gooseberry or rhubarb

GRILLED DUCK BREASTS

If you remember to marinate the breasts the night before this is then one of those quick and easy dishes which look so good!

2 or 3 duck breasts   NOTES
seasoning
3tbs honey
juice of a half lemon
juice of an orange
1dsp soy sauce
knob of fresh ginger
50g butter

Make shallow cuts through the breast skin and rub the seasoning in well. Grate the ginger.

In a shallow dish mix together the honey, lemon and orange juice, soy sauce and ginger. Thoroughly coat the breasts with this marinade and chill for a few hours or overnight, turning from time to time.

Remove the breasts from the marinade and pat dry. Under a hot grill, cook for 5 - 8 minutes each side (let the skinless side cook first) or until the skin is crispy and the flesh still just pink in the middle.

Meanwhile boil and reduce the marinade to a syrup. Off the heat whisk in the butter and serve with the duck breasts cut into thick slices.

TIPS AND VARIATIONS-

- Gressingham duck breasts are ideally bred for this dish
- make sure the duck breasts are really dry before marinating
- it helps to get the skin crisp if you start on a lower grill heat for a few minutes
- let the breasts 'rest' for a couple of minutes before slicing
- these will also barbeque very well
- goes well with new potatoes or couscous and a little gem salad

PORK SCHNITZEL

a very much tastier version of the well known wiener schnitzel

1 pork fillet

2-3 slices dry bread

2 eggs

2 tbs seasoned flour

1-2 cloves garlic

lemon

oil and butter

parsley

Cut the fillet across into 2" sections – you should have about 5 or 6 pieces. Using a kitchen mallet beat each piece of meat until about a ½" thick escalope. Put into a plastic bag with the seasoned flour and jiggle it around for a few moments until the meat is well coated.

Roughly chop the garlic and put into a food processor with the bread and whiz at high speed until you have nice garlicky breadcrumbs; put in a shallow bowl. In another bowl beat together the eggs.

Using your fingers, coat the floured meat evenly, first with the egg and then press well into the breadcrumbs. Set aside until ready to cook.

Put some oil and butter in a wide pan over a medium heat and when gently sizzling cook the pork escalopes for about 5-10 minutes each side until nicely golden and just cooked through.

Squeeze some lemon juice into the remaining butter in the pan and pour over the escalopes. Sprinkle with chopped parsley and serve with slices of lemon and a salad.

TIPS AND VARIATIONS-

* egging and breadcrumbing is a messy business, but licking your fingers afterwards is some compensation
* spice it up a bit by putting in some chilli when making the breadcrumbs
* you can of course use veal escalopes, when you will have a genuine Austrian wiener schnitzel viennoise

SHEPHERD'S PIE

*A very tasty variation on a homely dish, using a parsnip
topping; not everyone liked it, but I did, so here it is*

850g parsnips

2 medium onions

butter

½tsp each of ground cumin, coriander
and garam masala

2 medium leeks

2 medium carrots

250g mushrooms

500g minced lamb

1tbs flour

1tbs tomato purée

1dsp Worcestershire sauce

seasoning

250ml stock

NOTES

Cut the parsnips into large chunks and simmer in salted water until just tender, about 15 minutes. Drain and mash.

Slice the onions, chop the leeks, dice the carrots and slice the mushrooms. Grind the spices.

Simmer the onions in butter until soft, stir in the spices for a couple of minutes and then add the mashed parsnips with some black pepper and a little more butter to moisten.

In a large pan or wok gently cook the leeks and carrots in butter until soft and just colouring. Add the mushrooms and stir around for a few minutes and then stir in the minced lamb. Mix it all up until the meat starts to brown, stirring in the flour and tomato *purée*. Add the stock and let it simmer, uncovered, very gently for 20-30 minutes, stirring occasionally. Add the Worcestershire sauce and seasoning as it cooks.

In a large shallow dish spread the lamb mixture and cover with the mashed parsnips. Fluff up the surface with a fork, dot with butter, and bake in a medium oven for 25-30 minutes when the top should be a nice golden brown.

Tips and Variations-

* a cheaper and lean cut of lamb is best
* vary the amount of spices to your taste
* traditionally, of course, one uses potato for the topping; but try celeriac or swede or a mixture of any with potato
* spice up the topping with mustard or some grated cheese instead
* all can be prepared well in advance and refrigerated; and baked when ready
* you can use left over cooked lamb, but reduce the simmering stage
* you could use minced beef, but then of course it is a cottage pie!

SPICY LEG OF LAMB

This is a wonderfully impressive dish for a dinner party;
quite hard work but very rewarding – lamb in a rich and spicy sauce

large leg of lamb
2-3 medium onions
8-10 garlic cloves
2tbs almonds
large piece of fresh ginger
4 green chillies
500ml greek style yoghurt
2tbs coriander seeds
1tbs cumin seeds
1tsp cardamom seeds
2tsp turmeric
1tsp cayenne pepper
2 dsp garam masala
3tbs sultanas and a few more almonds

NOTES

Remove all the outside skin and fat from the lamb and take out the end bone – or get your butcher to do this – make a number of deep cuts into the meat on all sides.

Coarsely chop, and then blend, the onion, garlic, almonds, ginger and chilli into a paste.

Grind the cumin, cardamom and coriander and mix together with the yoghurt, cayenne, turmeric and garam masala into the onion paste.

Put the lamb into a suitably sized baking dish and spread the paste all over, rubbing it well into the cuts and cavities. Cover and chill for several hours or overnight.

Cover with aluminium foil, and bake in medium hot oven, c.200°C, for about 1½ hours. Remove the foil and cook uncovered for another 40 minutes, basting from time to time.

Scatter over the sultanas and remaining almonds and cook 5 more minutes. Put on a serving dish with the sauce spread around the leg and carve.

TIPS AND VARIATIONS-

* preferably grind all your own spices
* you can vary the spices to your liking and experiment

STEAK AND KIDNEY PUDDING

A traditional English classic, perfect on a cold winters day

500g stewing steak

200g ox kidney

medium onion

seasoned flour

Worcestershire sauce and seasoning

NOTES

FOR THE SUET PASTRY

300g self raising flour

150g shredded beef suet

½tsp each salt and pepper

about ½ pint cold water

You will need a 1½ pint pudding basin and a steamer

Make the pastry by sifting the flour and salt into a large mixing basin. Add the suet and pepper and mix with a fork. Add the water, little by little, mixing as you go until a dough is formed. By hand form into a ball, knead, and put on a floured board. Reserve a quarter for the lid and roll out the remainder into a circle. Grease the basin and line with the pastry up to and just over the top.

Cut the steak and kidney into 1" cubes – keep any fatty bits for gravy. Thinly slice the onion. Coat the meat cubes in the seasoned flour.

Fill the pudding basin with the meat and onion in alternate layers, sprinkle over 1-2tbs Worcestershire sauce and season. Fill with water so the meat is just not covered. Roll out the remaining pastry to form a lid, cover and seal.

Cover with greaseproof paper, secure with a rubber band, cover again with foil, pleating it and the paper in the middle to allow for expansion, and secure with string making a loop to use as a handle.

Put the basin into the steamer with an upturned plate underneath, so it does not touch the bottom. Half fill with boiling water and steam for around 4 hours, occasionally topping up the water.

Run a knife around the inside of the basin and carefully turn the pudding out onto a warm dish. Serve with mashed potatoes, peas and a rich gravy.

TIPS AND VARIATIONS-

* you could add 250g button mushrooms to the meat
* use beef stock rather than water to fill the pudding
* the easiest way to coat the meat with flour is to shake it all in a plastic bag

STUFFED CABBAGE

This is chou farçi, and although quite time consuming, is a fun dish to make on a cold winter's day

1 large savoy cabbage
400g pork sausage meat
150g chicken or lamb's liver
seasoning and mixed herbs
1 large onion
3 medium potatoes
2 large carrots
bay leaf
6tbs white wine
250ml stock
4 bacon rashers

NOTES

Wash the cabbage and discard the loose outer leaves. Put into boiling salted water and blanch for 5 minutes. Drain upside down in a colander.

Chop the chicken livers and mix together with the sausage meat, seasoning and herbs.

When the cabbage is cool enough to handle cut out the stalk. and open out the leaves like the petals of a flower. Cut out the heart and chop it finely into the meat mixture.

Insert the meat little by little between each cabbage leaf. Pull the leaves together to reform, and tie with string or tape.

Roughly slice the onion, potatoes and carrots. Put into a deep casserole. Place the cabbage, stalk end down, on top. Lay the bacon rashers across and pour over the wine and stock.

Cover the casserole and braise in a slow oven, c.135°C, for around 3 hours, basting from time to time. Serve the *chou farçi* surrounded with the carrots, potatoes and onions.

TIPS AND VARIATIONS-

* use sausage meat from a free range pig
* when blanching, the larger the pan of boiling water, the more quickly will it return to the boil
* allow plenty of time for opening up the cabbage leaves and the stuffing
* any left over fries up wonderfully as a 'bubble and squeak' next day
* try different mixed stuffings - chicken, salami, ham, bacon, mushrooms, red or green peppers, black olives, rice, etc.
* also try a red cabbage stuffed with apples, sultanas, onion and red peppers.
* use an egg to moisten a bit if your stuffing seems too dry

TWICE COOKED LEG OF LAMB WITH MASH

New Zealand lamb is ideal for this simple but succulent dish of braised lamb;
it has the advantage of being cooked in two parts, so can be prepared partially in advance

1 New Zealand leg of lamb

2-3 medium onions

2 large carrots

12 garlic cloves

2 bay leaves

bottle of New Zealand red wine

seasoning

NOTES

THE MASH

3 tbs olive oil

500g parsnips

1 leek

500g potatoes

50g butter

Quarter the onions and cut the carrots into chunks.

Put the lamb in a casserole. Surround with the onions, carrots, garlic cloves and bay leaves; pour in the red wine. Sprinkle over a dessertspoon of salt. Cover and bring to the boil, then simmer gently, in a slow oven, c.135°C, for about 90 minutes.

Remove the lamb, reserving the liquid and vegetables separately. Brush a roasting pan with oil, add the vegetables and place the lamb on top. Brush remaining oil over the top of the lamb and put in a medium hot oven, c.200°C, and roast for 45 minutes or so until tender.

Meanwhile chop the parsnips, potatoes and leeks into large chunks. Simmer in salted water until tender. Drain, mash with butter and season well with pepper.

Boil the reserved liquid and reduce to a coating consistency

Carve the lamb and serve on a bed of mash with the juices poured over.

TIPS AND VARIATIONS-

- if the lamb is frozen make sure it is thoroughly defrosted and dry
- vary the mash with celeriac, parsnip or onions etc.
- do not worry about using so much garlic – with long cooking it just leaves a wonderful aroma

WHITSUN LAMB

*A delicious combination of asparagus and lamb just
when the asparagus season starts and the spring lamb is best*

2 bunches asparagus

NOTES

750g lean lamb – leg or loin

flour

seasoning

pinch mustard

butter

2 medium onions

200ml chicken stock

125ml double cream

juice of a ½ lemon

Cut the lamb into chunky medallions, i.e. about 3" across by 1" thick. Thinly slice the onions. Break off and discard the tough stalks of the asparagus.

Coat the lamb pieces in seasoned flour by shaking together in a plastic bag. Gently fry the onions in butter in a large casserole until soft. Add the lamb and stir around for a few minutes until sealed and lightly browned.

Stir in the stock and bring to the boil. Simmer very gently either on the stove or in a slow oven for 40 minutes or so, until the lamb is just cooked and tender.

Meanwhile cook the asparagus in boiling salted water until *al dente*. Drain, cut off the tips and set on one side. Blend the stems in a liquidiser to a smooth *purée*.

Remove the lamb pieces from the casserole and arrange on a serving dish. Stir the cream and asparagus *purée* into the sauce remaining in the casserole, together with the lemon juice, a pinch of mustard and seasoning. Cook for a few minutes, stirring frequently, until you have a thick smooth sauce.

Pour the sauce over and around the meat and garnish with the asparagus tips.

Serve with new potatoes and spring vegetables.

Tips and Variations-

- if you push the asparagus stems through a sieve it makes for a smoother sauce
- do be careful not to overcook the lamb, it can so quickly toughen
- ideally remove all fat from the lamb

RÉCHAUFFÉS

Chicken croquettes with pineapple
Devilled turkey
Jambon Marie Rose
Miroton of beef
Moussaka
Pork croquettes
Pork meatloaf with tomato sauce
Russian salmon pie
Turkey, ham and mushroom pie

A *RÉCHAUFFÉ* IS A dish made from previously cooked cold ingredients, usually meat. i.e. the 'left overs' from Sunday lunches, Christmas and Easter and other such occasions when one inevitably cooks more food than is needed; such a shame to throw good food away or even to give it to the dog. So it is always useful to have a few good ideas to hand.

The most important rule to remember with *réchauffé* dishes is that the meat should not be cooked for a second time, otherwise it will become tough and stringy. A gentle reheating or a quick frying to seal the outside surfaces is the most that is needed.

Bubble and squeak, although not meat, is of course a classic *réchauffé* being simply chopped up cold cooked potato (roast, baked, mashed or boiled) mixed up with cold chopped cabbage or sprouts and fried as a large patty in oil or butter, with perhaps some chopped garlic or onion for extra zing.

These are mostly fairly simple recipes but with care and some thought you can make some really interesting and unusual meals, and have the satisfaction of not wasting good food or previous effort. Of course you could make any of these dishes by cooking the ingredients from scratch, but that would entirely defeat the object!

CHICKEN CROQUETTES
WITH PINEAPPLE

This is a simple but homely version of croquettes, but again a brilliant way to make use of left-over chicken or turkey. The sharpness of the pineapple makes a refreshing contrast.

3-400g cooked chicken

2 slices dry bread

bunch of spring onions

large egg

seasoning

tin of pineapple slices in syrup

lemon

butter

3 tbs brown sugar

NOTES

Chop the chicken into very small pieces (rather than mincing). Marinate for an hour or two in the pineapple juice from the tin.

Process the bread into crumbs. Finely chop the onions. Grate the zest from the lemon, squeeze and save its juice.

Strain the chicken, saving the juice. Mix the diced chicken with the onion, lemon rind and seasoning and bind with the egg. Add enough breadcrumbs to make it reasonably firm.

By hand, make four small cakes with the mixture. Arrange each cake on a pineapple slice and put in a greased baking tin.

Melt a knob of butter in a pan, add the brown sugar and the juice from the pineapple and lemon. Stir well and when blended pour over the croquettes.

Bake in a moderate oven for 30-40 minutes – baste with the juices from time to time.

TIPS AND VARIATIONS-

- pork, turkey or pheasant will do just as well
- use herbs instead of the spring onions
- *crème fraîche* would go rather well with this
- instead of spring onion fry up some chopped onion and mushroom
- use fresh pineapple

DEVILLED TURKEY

A traditional treat and a highlight of a Boxing Day breakfast

750g of cooked turkey meat

NOTES

MARINADE INGREDIENTS-
125ml sunflower oil
2tbs Worcestershire sauce
2tbs tomato ketchup
1dsp English mustard
1dsp french mustard
2tsps sugar
a few drops of anchovy essence
seasoning
½tsp cayenne

Thoroughly mix all the marinade ingredients together. Cut the meat into largish pieces, removing any skin.

Lay the meat in the marinade and spoon over the juices making sure that all parts are coated. Leave to marinate for several hours, basting from time to time.

Under a hot grill cook the turkey pieces for 12-15 minutes, turning once.

Serve with fried tomato halves, mushrooms, bacon and a watercress garnish.

TIPS AND VARIATIONS-
- use any parts of the turkey including bones with meat attached
- making some slashes in the meat helps the marinade penetrate
- alternatively cook in a hot oven for 15 minutes
- any poultry can be devilled like this, but goose is particularly delicious

JAMBON MARIE ROSE

A rich and attractive way to make use of surplus Christmas ham (and Madeira if any!)

4 thick slices of cooked ham

oil and butter

2tbs finely chopped onion

1 tbs flour

125ml chicken stock

5tbs Madeira or medium sherry

1tps tomato purée

black pepper

125ml double cream

spinach and parsley

NOTES

In a large frying pan fry the ham slices quickly in a little oil and butter, one or two at a time, until lightly browned and then set aside.

Leave some fat in the pan and gently cook the onion until just soft. Stir in the flour and cook for a few minutes.

Meanwhile separately bring the stock and madeira to the boil and blend into the onions and flour. Add the tomato *purée* and pepper and simmer for a few minutes gradually stirring in the cream; continue to simmer until it has a light coating consistency, stirring all the while.

Check seasoning, add the ham slices and reheat gently. Serve on a bed of chopped cooked spinach and decorate with chopped parsley.

TIPS AND VARIATIONS-

- use *crème fraîche* or yoghurt in place of cream

MIROTON OF BEEF

A simple and very tasty way to make good use of left over roast beef

500g cold roast beef

3 medium onions

fat or butter

dsp flour

125ml stock, or more

glass white wine

3-4 cloves garlic

bay leaf and seasoning

750g potatoes

lemon juice

breadcrumbs

NOTES

Boil the potatoes in their jackets until just cooked and allow to cool. Slice the onions thinly, blanch for 3-4 minutes in boiling water and drain thoroughly. Slice the beef as finely as you can. Crush and chop the garlic cloves.

Heat some fat in a pan and cook the drained onions for a few minutes until lightly browned. Dust in the flour and stir around. Add the wine and enough stock so that when the flour is absorbed you have an onion sauce of coating consistency. Add the bay leaf, garlic and season to taste. Cover and simmer gently for 20 minutes. Allow to cool.

Stir the beef into the sauce as it cools and add a squeeze or two of lemon juice.

Thickly slice the cooked potatoes and arrange *en couronne* in an ovenproof dish. Put the beef slices and sauce within the ring of potatoes. Sprinkle over the breadcrumbs and dot with butter. Brown quickly in a hot oven – about 15 minutes.

TIPS AND VARIATIONS-

- there are many variations on this recipe, but this one is the best
- you may already have some left over roast potatoes so use these
- if you leave any fat on the beef it makes for a richer *miroton*
- the dish can be made well beforehand and finished in the oven just before eating
- use cider instead of wine
- *miroton* translates from the french as 'boiled in an onion sauce'!

MOUSSAKA

There are very many different recipes for this dish, some using beef and others lamb.
This one makes good use of the left over roast lamb from Sunday lunch

500g cold cooked lamb

olive oil and butter

2 medium onions

seasoning

tomato ketchup

125g potatoes

aubergine

several garlic cloves

tin tomatoes

250ml cheese sauce

egg and grated cheese

NOTES

Cut the lamb into bite size pieces. Roughly chop one onion and slice the other, peel and thinly slice the potatoes, crush the garlic and slice the aubergine thickly.

Soften the onions in the oil and butter in a wide pan, add the lamb and stir around for a few minutes. Season well and add enough ketchup to moisten – set aside in an 8/10" baking dish and keep warm.

Fry the potato slices in more oil and butter until lightly browned, and just cooked through, and arrange on top of the meat.

Fry the aubergine slices in the remaining oil, add the garlic and tomatoes and cook for 5-10 minutes. Then cover the potatoes with this mixture.

Meanwhile prepare a cheese sauce in the usual way and stir in the egg. It should have a thick creamy consistency. Pour this over the dish and sprinkle with the grated cheese.

Bake in a medium oven for 15-20 minutes until browned on top and ready to serve.

TIPS AND VARIATIONS-

- any flavoursome bottled sauce may be used to moisten the meat
- this dish reheats very well
- try substituting Jerusalem artichokes or courgettes for the aubergine
- you could blanch the aubergine slices instead of frying
- slice left over roast potatoes from your Sunday lunch – no need to fry

PORK CROQUETTES

Croquettes are a wonderful way of using up left over cold meats to create a seriously good dish
Pork is one of the best, but there can be many variations

1tbs flour
butter
medium onion
250ml stock

300g cooked pork
125g bacon
chopped parsley
pinch nutmeg
seasoning
egg yolk

flour, egg and breadcrumbs
more butter
parsley and lemon

NOTES

Finely chop the onion and soften in the butter. Add the flour, cook for a few minutes and stir in the stock to make a thick sauce. Allow to cool.

Chop the pork and bacon. Then mix in with the sauce and chopped parsley, nutmeg, egg yolk and seasoning. Refrigerate until chilled and firm to handle – an hour or so.

Have ready three small bowls with the flour, the beaten egg and the breadcrumbs. By hand make the chilled pork mixture into 4 or 5 firmly shaped flattish portions, squeezing gently as you do it.

Coat each portion with flour, dip into the beaten egg and then coat with the breadcrumbs, pressing these gently onto the croquettes.

Shallow fry in butter for a few minutes each side until lightly browned. Drain on absorbent kitchen paper. Serve garnished with sliced lemon and parsley.

TIPS AND VARIATIONS-

- a few drops of oil added to the beaten eggs helps the breadcrumbs to stick
- try adding some finely chopped garlic or chilli to the breadcrumbs
- it may be easier to mince the meat but not so good as chopping
- beef and lamb work well – but they are better spiced up a bit.
- chicken or turkey are good, but better using a slightly different version of croquettes – *see chicken croquettes page 106.*

A PORK MEATLOAF SOUFFLÉ
WITH TOMATO SAUCE

*A wonderful way to use leftovers from a roast which can mostly be made
well in advance, but you will need a mincer with a fine disc*

400g cooked pork

3 garlic cloves

handful of parsley

8-10 black olives

200ml milk

4 egg yolks

6 egg whites

1tsp lemon juice

NOTES

FOR THE TOMATO SAUCE

medium onion

1 tbs olive oil

1 clove garlic

300g chopped tinned tomatoes

2tsps dried mixed herbs

2tbs tomato purée

Firstly make the tomato sauce. Finely chop the onion and crush the garlic. Sweat the onion in the oil for a few minutes until softening. Add the tomatoes, garlic and herbs. Cover and cook gently for 5-10 minutes. Add the *purée* and 200ml water and simmer, uncovered, for 30 minutes. Season to taste and liquidize until smooth, or pass through a sieve. Reserve until later.

Roughly chop the meat and mince finely. Put the garlic and the parsley through the mincer, followed by a little bread to make sure it all comes through. Chop the olives. Add the egg yolks, milk and seasoning. Mix very thoroughly and check for seasoning.

Whisk the egg whites into soft peaks, add the lemon juice and a pinch of salt, and whisk until firm peaks are reached.

Put about one third of the egg whites into the meat mixture and stir very thoroughly. Carefully fold in the remaining egg whites.

Butter an appropriately sized *soufflé* dish and put in the mixture. Cook in a *bain marie* in a medium oven, c.190°C, for 45-50 minutes.

Carefully turn out the *soufflé* onto a serving dish, pour over the reheated tomato sauce, sprinkle with chopped parsley and serve.

TIPS AND VARIATIONS-
* you can make this dish with cooked beef, lamb or veal, or even cooked fish such as salmon
* it can be easier to make in four individual *soufflé* dishes

RUSSIAN SALMON PIE

More properly known as 'Coulibiac de Saumon', this is a French adaption of a classic Russian recipe, much easier to make than it appears and it looks very good.

400g cooked salmon   NOTES

125g butter

1tbs flour

200ml milk

medium onion

250g mushrooms

2 eggs

seasoning

250g made puff pastry

beaten egg to glaze

Divide the salmon into largish pieces, discarding any skin or bone. Hard boil the eggs and cut in pieces. Finely chop the onion and slice the mushrooms.

Make a thick *béchamel* sauce with half the butter, the flour and the milk. Cook the onion and mushroom for a few minutes in the remaining butter until softened. Then stir them into the sauce with the egg and seasoning to taste. Let the sauce mixture cool.

Roll out the pastry on a lightly floured board as thinly as you can. Spread over half the cooled sauce mixture and put the salmon pieces on top. Cover with remaining sauce. Damp the pastry edges to 'seal' and fold over to form a 'bolster'.

Brush with the beaten egg to form a glaze and score with criss cross patterns to prettify.

Bake the pie in a medium hot oven for 30-40 minutes until crisp and golden.

TIPS AND VARIATIONS-
- a few chopped herbs never go amiss
- add a few freshly cooked peas or broad beans
- this is so good that you are quite justified in cooking a piece of fresh salmon rather than using 'left overs'!

TURKEY, HAM AND MUSHROOM PIE

A splendidly simple way to use up surplus post Christmas ham and turkey.
The carcase of the bird makes a lovely rich stock – it will moisten even dried out turkey meat

500g turkey meat
250g ham
250g button mushrooms
2 medium onions
1 tbs flour
250ml turkey stock
pkt of frozen puff pastry
1 egg
seasoning
butter

NOTES

Cut the turkey and ham into bite size pieces. Slice one onion and chop the other.

Quickly brown the mushrooms, whole, in a little butter until nearly cooked and all fat absorbed.

Separately soften all the onions in butter, add flour and stir for a few minutes, add stock and stir until creamy. Season well. It should be a thickish onion sauce. Let it cool awhile.

In a large pan combine the turkey and ham, the mushrooms and the sauce. Pack into an appropriately sized pie dish.

Roll out the unfrozen pastry and cover the dish, sealing the edges with a little water. Decorate with bits of surplus pastry and brush over the beaten egg.

Bake in a medium oven for 30-40 minutes until nicely browned on top.

TIPS AND VARIATIONS-

* use both white and brown turkey meat
* chicken can obviously be substituted for the turkey
* a few cooked carrots or peas will make it look pretty
* try using some finely sliced leeks instead of the sliced onions
* you can prepare the pie several hours beforehand and then cook when ready
* it's not a bad idea to make a little extra sauce in case the dish is too dry

CASSEROLES

A spicy lamb and bean casserole
Blanquette de veau
Braised Greek style lamb
Braised stuffed lambs' hearts
Fabada Asturiana
Faisan au choux
Jugged hare
Kidney and sausage casserole
Lapin Brabançonne
Navarin of lamb
Pheasant with apples
Pigeon casserole

THE WORD 'CASSEROLE', as with 'terrine', can mean either the vessel used for cooking or the contents themselves; or indeed as a verb to describe the method of cooking. As a method of cooking it goes back to very ancient times when it was first realised that long and slow cooking in a sealed, or tightly lidded , clay pot would soften tough and fibrous meats into a succulent and digestible meal.

These cuts of meat were the least valued parts of an animal and so inevitably casseroling was the preserve of the peasant and the less well off rural communities where there also tended to be a fire burning all and every day. From the British stew pot to the tagines of Morocco or the mud encrusted 'beggar's chicken' of eastern China the impoverished of the world learnt how to make the most of what little they had.

Although of humble origins some casseroles, when well and properly made, can reach the heights of culinary delight. A good jugged hare, blanquette de veau or navarin of lamb, for example, are quite exquisite.

Everyone has their own favourite casserole recipes and these are a few of mine. I have included some braised recipes which most conveniently fit in here. Many of the dishes are in effect a complete meal in one pot, and so, with the advantage of generally being able to be prepared in advance, are ideal for entertaining large numbers of people. In fact with most of them the flavour of the food will naturally improve if made a day or two beforehand and then gently reheated.

A SPICY LAMB AND BEAN CASSEROLE

A very good dish to prepare in advance for a large party

350g dried beans – kidney, flageolet, black eye etc

750g lean lamb

flour

olive oil

seasoning

250g button mushrooms

2 medium onions

4 garlic cloves

1tbs garam masala

250g dried apricots

500ml stock

yoghurt and parsley to garnish

NOTES

Soak the beans overnight or for several hours until fully swollen. Drain and rinse, then simmer in fresh water for 10-15 minutes when they should be soft but firm.

Slice the onions and chop the garlic. Roughly chop the apricots. Cut the lamb into 1" cubes and coat with seasoned flour.

In a large *sauté* pan, using a little oil over a fairly high heat, quickly brown the meat in batches, so that it does not stew, and remove to a large lidded casserole.

Lower the heat and brown the mushrooms – add to the casserole. Soften the onions and garlic, stir in the garam masala , add the stock, bring to the boil and add to the casserole.

Drain the beans and add to the casserole with the apricots.

Bring the casserole up to a slow simmer and taste for and adjust seasoning. Cover and put in a slow oven, c.165°C, for 1½-2 hours.

TIPS AND VARIATIONS-
- the easiest way to 'flour' the cubed meat is to put it into a plastic bag with some seasoned flour and shake it around
- serve with new potatoes and a green salad
- it almost improves with reheating and so can be prepared well in advance
- by doubling, trebling the quantities, or more, a large party can easily be fed

BLANQUETTE DE VEAU

A classic and delicately flavoured stew made from the cheaper cuts of veal

750g breast or shoulder of veal

salt and half a lemon

bouquet garni

sliced carrot and onion

seasoning

50g butter

1tbs flour

egg yolk

125ml cream

NOTES

Cut the meat into 1" cubes and put into a pan with a slice of lemon, and salted cold water to cover. Slowly bring just to the boil (this blanches and whitens the meat). Drain and rinse.

Put the rinsed meat into a saucepan with the *bouquet garni*, onion and carrot, just cover with fresh water. Cover and simmer very gently for an hour or so until the meat is just tender.

Strain off the meat, discard the vegetables but reserve the liquid.

Melt the butter in a pan, add the flour and stir for a few minutes, then add about 350ml of the reserved liquid and stir and cook for a few minutes until you have a smooth sauce.

Separately blend the egg yolk with the cream and add gradually back into the sauce whisking all the time. Add a teaspoon of lemon juice and check the seasoning.

Replace the veal in the sauce and heat through very gently - do not let it boil.

Serve decorated with chopped parsley or coriander.

TIPS AND VARIATIONS-

- a '*bouquet garni*' is a small tied bunch of parsley, thyme and a bay leaf
- a garnish of sliced mushrooms, peas and fried bread triangles is correct
- whilst this dish seems easy there are many things to go wrong – it is very easy to over cook the meat which should become meltingly tender – the sauce can curdle when the cream is added – if the seasonings are not right it can taste very bland

BRAISED LAMB GREEK STYLE

This is a typically 'peasant' type of dish which you will find all around the Mediterranean

shoulder of lamb

10-12 medium carrots

8 medium onions, red and white

5-6 fat garlic cloves

lots of seasoning

3-4 sprigs rosemary

NOTES

The shoulder needs to be cut through the bone into four or five pieces. Ask your butcher to do this for you or use a hacksaw. Halve the carrots crossways, slice two of the onions and roughly chop the garlic.

Brown the lamb pieces in a very hot pan so that at least some of the fat is melted. Remove the lamb and in the fat briefly brown the carrots and the six whole onions.

Put the carrots and whole onions into a large casserole and scatter over the garlic and the sliced onions. Put the lamb pieces on top in a single layer and season liberally. Roast, uncovered, in a very hot oven for about 30 minutes.

Remove everything from the casserole and pour off all the fat.

Put all the vegetables back into the casserole with the lamb on top and the rosemary. Cover and cook in a slow oven until the meat is falling from the bone. Probably two and a half hours or so.

Pour off all the juices and skim off the fat. You can make a gravy with this if you wish.

Serve on a large platter with the lamb on top of the vegetables.

TIPS AND VARIATIONS-

- lamb shoulder is quite fatty so it is important to remove as much of it as possible
- reheats well and so can be prepared in advance
- you can add so many things to this basically very simple dish; olives, herbs, potatoes, other root vegetables, celery etc
- you could of course use lamb shanks, but that's not what the greek peasants would have done

BRAISED STUFFED LAMBS HEARTS

*Not everybody's cup of tea this, but it brings back childhood memories of many
money saving dishes. The heart meat is actually quite delicately bland,
so it needs a flavoursome stuffing and the red currant jelly*

4 lambs hearts

sage and onion stuffing

carrots

onions

celery

stock

seasoning

red currant jelly

NOTES

Wash the hearts and soak in salted water for 1-2 hours. Thickly slice the carrots, onions and celery. Use a sharp knife or scissors to cut out the tubes from the hearts.

Make the stuffing by mixing together, 20 finely chopped sage leaves, 1tbs suet, a medium onion finely chopped and softened in butter, 2 slices bread crumbed, seasoning and a beaten egg.

Push as much stuffing as you can into the cavities in the hearts and use cocktail sticks to hold it all in. Put into a casserole dish on top of the chopped vegetables. Season well.

Pour in enough stock to cover the vegetables, plus a little. Cook in a slow to medium oven, c.160-180°C, for about 1½ hours, basting with the stock from time to time.

Remove the hearts and vegetables and keep warm. Reduce the stock, or thicken, to make a gravy and serve the lambs hearts with the vegetables, some new potatoes and the red currant jelly.

TIPS AND VARIATIONS-

- use a packet of ready made stuffing
- an anchovy stuffing might be good
- make any left over stuffing into stuffing balls
- you could cook for longer in a slower oven
- this one does not reheat at all well!

FABADA ASTURIANA

This spicy bean and sausage peasant stew is quite delicious; it is widely available in Spain, but is a speciality of the Asturias region in the North

250g cannelloni, haricot or butter beans

2 medium onions

4-5 cloves garlic

olive oil

400g tin of chopped tomatoes

seasoning

pinch of saffron or ½ tsp turmeric

125g piece smoked bacon

250g black pudding

250g chorizo sausage

2 bay leaves

handful spinach leaves

NOTES

Soak the beans for several hours or overnight. Drain, cover with cold water, bring to the boil and simmer for 5-10 minutes. Drain again and set aside.

Coarsely chop the onions; crush and chop the garlic; cut the bacon, chorizo and black pudding into pieces, so that you have one or two pieces each per person.

Gently fry the onion and garlic in oil until softening. Stir in the tomatoes, saffron or turmeric, bay leaves and seasoning and cook for a few minutes.

Add the beans, bacon, chorizo and black pudding. Just cover with water and bring to the boil. Cover and put in a very slow oven, about 135°C, and let it simmer away gently for 1½ hours or so, until the beans are tender.

Stir in the spinach leaves 20-30 minutes before serving with lots of crusty bread.

TIPS AND VARIATIONS-
* you could use tinned beans to avoid the overnight soaking
* the black pudding will dissolve; if preferred whole put in half way through

FAISAN AUX CHOUX

This braised pheasant dish is a simple to prepare, very succulent,
and the somewhat unlikely combination of flavours is remarkably good

pheasant
large savoy cabbage
large onion
2 celery sticks
250g belly pork or gammon
butter and seasoning

NOTES

Slice the cabbage fairly thinly, chop half the onion and slice the other half, thinly slice the celery and dice the belly pork.

Sauté the onion, celery and belly pork in butter for a few minutes in a large casserole. Add the cabbage and stir frequently until it begins to turn golden, or for 10-15 minutes

Season well and add 4 tablespoons water. Cover and simmer very gently for 20-30 minutes.

Meanwhile, in another pan, brown the pheasant all over in butter.

Put the pheasant in the casserole surrounded and covered by the cabbage mixture; cook in a slow oven, c.135°C, for about 2 hours until the pheasant is just tender.

Carve the pheasant and serve on a bed of the braised cabbage.

Tips and Variations-
- This also works very well with partridges - *'perdrix aux choux'*, a french classic
- also good with a chicken
- try using leeks instead of cabbage
- you can use bacon instead of belly pork
- you can use a white cabbage, but savoy is better

JUGGED HARE

One of the classic game dishes – essential parts are the liaison with the blood to thicken the sauce, its enrichment with port and the accompanying force-meat balls

1 hare – well hung

2 onions and cloves

celery stick and carrot

bouquet garni and 1tsp allspice

butter and seasoning

juice of a lemon

1-2 pints stock

large glass of port

1tbs red currant jelly

beurre manié

blood of hare

MARINADE

½ bottle red wine

3tbs olive oil

sliced shallot

2 bay leaves

seasoning

crushed juniper berries

NOTES

Make the marinade by putting all its ingredients together, bring to the boil and cool.

Skin and draw the hare; make sure to reserve the blood collected in a membrane in the rib cage. Divide into 12-14 portion sized pieces. Cover with the marinade for 4-5 hours or overnight.

Quarter the onions and stick with the cloves; slice the celery and quarter the carrot.

Remove and dry the pieces of hare, reserving the marinade. Brown them quickly in butter and pack into a casserole with the onion, celery, carrot, bouquet, seasoning, allspice and lemon juice.

Just cover with stock, put on the lid and bring to the boil. Put in a slow oven, c.135°C, and let simmer gently for 2-3 hours until the meat is very tender, almost falling from the bone. Carefully remove the pieces onto a serving dish and keep warm.

Strain the cooking liquor, discarding the vegetables, and thicken with enough *beurre manié* to give a creamy consistency. Remove from the heat and make the liaison with the blood – slowly add several spoonfuls of liquor to the blood, stirring, then pour it back carefully into the remaining liquor with the port and red currant jelly. The sauce should be rich and very smooth.

Pour the sauce over the hare and serve, very hot, with force-meat balls – see page 188.

TIPS AND VARIATIONS-
- preparation of the hare is not for the squeamish - ask your butcher, or a friend to do this – but make sure the blood is reserved
- if you don't have, or can't face, the blood, use some of the strained marinade
- the french version of this dish is *Civet de Lièvre* which differs in that chunks of bacon, baby onions, garlic and mushrooms are cooked with the hare. The important blood liaison is similar but they garnish with fried bread triangles instead of force-meat balls. Sounds more like *coq au vin* to me!

KIDNEY AND SAUSAGE CASSEROLE

A tasty and homely dish which can be made well in advance and reheated.
Best using fresh lambs' kidneys and good quality sausages

6-8 lambs' kidneys
250g small sausages
2 medium onions
50g butter
1 tbs flour
250ml chicken stock
250ml red wine
2 tbs tomato purée
seasoning
250g button mushrooms
120g frozen peas

NOTES

Cut the kidneys in half and squeeze and twist the sausages into little balls. Slice the onions.

Fry the onion in butter, gently, until softening. Add the kidneys and sausages and stir fry for a few minutes to seal. Remove all to a casserole dish leaving the butter and juices in the pan.

Add the flour to the buttery juices in the pan and over a gentle heat, stir for a few minutes; slowly add the stock, wine and tomato *purée* – season well and simmer for a few minutes until you have a medium coating sauce.

Pour the sauce over the sausages and kidneys in the casserole dish and stir. Cover and put in a slow oven for an hour or so.

Slice the mushrooms and add them, with the frozen peas, 30 minutes after putting in the oven.

Remove from the oven and keep warm until ready to serve.

TIPS AND VARIATIONS-

* goes well with rice, couscous or mashed potato and a green salad
* use big fat mushrooms, quartered, and put in sooner
* add bacon bits to the initial fry to make a richer stew
* the flavours will improve with reheating, but take care not to overcook
* if no stock, or cubes, are available water, (or more wine!), works just as well

LAPIN BRABANÇONNE

This rabbit casserole should convince anyone who might have been a bit dubious about eating rabbit just what a wonderfully tasty, and economical, dish it can be

1 rabbit

150g piece of bacon or gammon

fat or butter

2 tbs flour

3-4 medium onions

up to 1 pint of beer

2-3 slices bread

french mustard

seasoning

2 tsps sugar

NOTES

Joint the rabbit into 7 or 8 pieces and soak in salted water with a little vinegar, for several hours or overnight. Drain and pat dry.

Cut the bacon into thick strips, halve and slice the onions. Spread mustard generously on one side of the bread. Coat the rabbit pieces in seasoned flour by shaking in a plastic bag.

Heat the fat in a casserole or a wide lidded *sauté* pan. Brown the bacon with the onion. Remove and quickly brown the rabbit pieces in the remaining fat.

Drain off any surplus fat and put the bacon and onion back on top of the rabbit pieces. Sprinkle over the sugar. Cover with the slices of mustard spread bread, mustard side down. Pour in the beer to just below the level of the bread.

Cover and cook in a very slow oven for 1½ hours or so, when the meat should be just beginning to fall from the bone. Serve from the casserole.

TIPS AND VARIATIONS-

- the marinating of the rabbit is important as it enhances the flavour and, apparently, makes it more digestible
- if the juices seem too thin it may be worth pouring off and reducing
- perhaps add a handful of sultanas or prepared prunes for the last half hour
- a sprinkling of chopped parsley will prettify things

NAVARIN OF LAMB

Sweetly delicious when made with young spring vegetables and new season lamb

750g boned shoulder of lamb

2tbs olive oil

2 tsps sugar

2tbs seasoned flour

300ml stock or water

1tbs tomato purée

3 garlic cloves

bouquet of bay leaf, thyme and parsley

8 small onions

4 carrots

4 medium new potatoes

250g peas

NOTES

Cut the meat into 1½" cubes. Crush the garlic. Quarter the carrots and the potatoes.

Coat the lamb with flour by shaking in a plastic bag. Heat the oil in a wide pan or wok and fry the meat for a few minutes until lightly browned. Drain off any excess fat. Sprinkle sugar over the meat and stir until lightly caramelised.

Put the meat into a casserole dish and stir in the stock, tomato *purée*, garlic and herbs. Bring to the boil, cover and simmer very gently for 30 minutes. Add the vegetables, bring back to the boil and simmer for about 1 hour or until the meat is just tender. Add peas for the last 5-10 minutes.

TIPS AND VARIATIONS-

- the whole art of this dish is to get everything cooked just right at the same time
- include other spring vegetables; french beans, broad beans, turnips, shallots, whole garlic cloves etc as you will
- a Navarin should be served with hot french bread and a good chilled *rosé* wine

PHEASANT WITH APPLES

Faisan à la Vallée d'Auge
This is a rich Normandy casserole of complementing flavours

1 young pheasant
oil and butter
medium onion
4 good eating apples
3tbs calvados or brandy
150ml cider
300ml double cream
seasoning
handful of parsley

NOTES

Finely chop the onion. Peel and core the apples. Slice three apples and cut the other into rings. Chop the parsley.

In a suitably sized casserole slowly brown the pheasant all over in oil and butter. Add the onions and cook for some minutes longer. Drain off any surplus fat.

Heat the calvados in a small pan and pour over the pheasant. Set alight. When the flames die down, add the cider, sliced apples, cream and seasoning.

Cover and simmer gently for about 50-60 minutes or until the pheasant is just cooked through.

Carve the pheasant and arrange on a serving dish. Sieve, or liquidise, the apple sauce and boil rapidly until reduced to a coating consistency. Briefly fry the apple rings.

Pour the sauce over the pheasant and garnish with the fried apple rings and parsley.

Tips and Variations-
- chicken is also very good done this way
- the pheasant will cook more evenly if the legs are spread rather than trussed
- cooking apples can be used – it just tastes a little tarter
- as with most casseroles it reheats well as long as you don't let the meat dry out
- it can be easier to brown the pheasant first in a frying pan whilst softening the onions in the casserole.
- I tend to use longlife cream as fresh can often curdle

PIGEON CASSEROLE

*People can be quite funny about pigeon, but I would rate it more highly than
any game bird, when well cooked, and simmered in red wine it is really delicious*

4 pigeons

200g bacon or gammon

12 button onions

250g button mushrooms

3-4 garlic cloves

olive oil and butter

dried mixed herbs

seasoning

½ bottle red wine

NOTES

Cut the bacon into modest sized chunks. Crush and chop the garlic.

Quickly brown the pigeons all over in oil and butter in a large pan, followed by the bacon and onions and remove to a casserole.

Add the garlic, herbs and seasoning to the casserole, cover and cook over a low heat for ten minutes. Add the wine and when just simmering, cover and move to a slow oven.

Let it cook very gently for 1½ hours or so - add the mushrooms after 45 minutes. When the meat is tender remove and arrange on a serving dish. Keep warm.

Reduce the remaining sauce to a coating consistency – or thicken it if you wish – pour over the pigeons and decorate with chopped parsley.

Tips and Variations-

- for a more elegant presentation, cut off the legs and wings and slice away the backbone so you just cook the breasts joined by the breastbone
- if you have young pigeons – squabs – it is best to just simply roast them
- use half stock, half wine if you don't like too winey a taste

CURRY and SPICE

A simple chicken curry
A more sophisticated chicken curry
Bombay pork with lentils
Brown lentils with onion and garlic
Cauliflower florets
Curried cauliflower pilaff
Lamb curry
Merguez sausages or burgers
Minced pork curry
Persian lamb polo
Sausage jambalaya
Spicy aubergine pieces
Spicy tuna with pasta

THERE ARE MANY good books on this subject, but so many recipes just seem to be only a variation on a theme; as do the menus in so many Indian restaurants!

Here are just a few of the recipes I have enjoyed cooking and which give a flavour of what can be achieved with spices. Curry pastes of quality are now readily available, such as Balti, Madras, Korma, Tandoori etc; they make simple curry dishes a doddle to prepare, and it is not cheating to do so. Although to buy and use a ready made curry sauce definitely is cheating! and really not very worthwhile.

However it is great fun to grind the spices oneself. All you need is a spice grinder – which is really just a cheap electric coffee grinder, and does the job perfectly. Whole spices keep for ages and only release their aroma when ground; whereas ground spices, bought in very expensive little bottles, lose it very quickly. Dry fry spices before grinding to give a more intense flavour, for example.

A good list of spices to have available would include – cumin, coriander, cardamom, fenugreek, mustard and fennel seeds; cloves, cinnamon sticks, nutmeg and turmeric. Onions, garlic, ginger and chillies are all essential; as are leaves of coriander, parsley and mint. Garam masala, regularly called for either to add to a dish or to flavour it later, is easily made – see page 189.

For a basic curry paste merely liquidise onions, ginger and garlic with a little water. Grind some whole seeds of, for example, cumin, coriander and cardamom into a powder and mix into the onion paste, perhaps with a little tomato puree – hey presto, in a matter of moments you have made your own curry paste – the basis of most curry dishes.

Chicken and pork are the easiest meats to curry; beef is tricky and fish needs a very delicate touch. But pretty well any vegetable will be delicious.

With a little imagination, experimentation and the blending of different spices, it is probably easier to be more creative than with any other style of cooking.

A SIMPLE CHICKEN CURRY

There are myriads of ways to make a good curry –
you can have a lot of fun grinding your own spices –
but this dish, using a curry paste, is quick to make and very good

500g skinless chicken breast

2 medium onions

2-3 fat garlic cloves

knob of root ginger

vegetable oil

2tbs curry paste (any good proprietary
brand)

2-3 large mushrooms

dollop of crème fraîche or greek yoghurt

seasoning

NOTES

Slice the onions thinly and then very thinly the garlic and ginger. Cut the chicken into large chunks and quarter the mushrooms.

Gently fry the onions in the oil in a large pan – a wok is ideal – until softened. Stir in the garlic and ginger and then the curry paste, cooking for a few more minutes.

Add the chicken pieces and stir round for a few moments until the meat is just sealed. Add 2-3 tablespoons of water and the mushrooms. Cover and simmer for 15-20 minutes, or until the chicken is just cooked.

Towards the end of the cooking time stir in the *crème fraîche* and seasoning.

Serve with couscous or rice and a green salad.

TIPS AND VARIATIONS-

- free range chicken is always better, but with a spicy or strongly flavoured dish the difference is not so apparent
- skinless chicken tends to absorb the flavours better than skin on
- you could add a ½ tin of chopped tomatoes
- if you have any spinach leaves, a few put in towards the end add interest

A MORE SOPHISTICATED
CHICKEN CURRY

*In Indian cookery terms this would probably be considered quite a
'simple' dish but for an amateur the combination of spicy flavours is exceptional.*

3 or 4 skinless chicken breasts

3 medium onions

2" piece fresh ginger

3 garlic cloves

sunflower oil

1tbs ground coriander seeds

1tbs ground cumin

1tsp turmeric

½tsp cayenne pepper

3-4tbs yoghurt

½ tin chopped tomatoes

1tsp salt

1-2tsps garam masala

chopped coriander or parsley

NOTES

Cut each breast into 3 or 4 pieces. Coarsely chop half of the onions, the ginger and garlic, and finely slice the remaining onions. Grind the spices if using whole seeds.

Liquidise the coarsely chopped onion, garlic and ginger with a little water, into a smooth paste.

Stir fry the sliced onions in a little oil, over a medium heat, until browning and almost crisp. Reserve.

Stir fry the paste in the remaining oil, with a little more oil if necessary, for 3 or 4 minutes. Add the spices, coriander, cumin, turmeric and cayenne and some of the yoghurt. Stir together adding the chicken pieces and the rest of the yoghurt.

Add the tomatoes and salt and enough water to give a thin creamy consistency. Cover and simmer over a gentle heat for 15-20 minutes.

Sprinkle over the garam masala and fried sliced onions and cook, uncovered, over a slightly higher heat for some 10 minutes, when the sauce should have thickened and the chicken is just cooked through. Garnish with the chopped fresh herbs.

TIPS AND VARIATIONS-
- grind your own spices if you have a spice/coffee grinder
- sunflower or vegetable oil generally seem better than olive oil with curry dishes
- the chicken is cooked without being browned or sealed first which gives it a rather different texture
- to make garam masala see page 189.

BOMBAY PORK WITH RED LENTILS

A wonderful winter warmer or, indeed, for any other time of year

150g split red lentils

2 medium onions

½ a green chilli

3 tsps whole cumin seeds

½ tsp turmeric

large knob of ginger

600g lean pork leg meat

1½ tsps salt

sunflower oil

2-4 cloves garlic

½tsp cayenne pepper

juice of half a lemon

½tsp sugar

1 tsp garam masala

NOTES

Coarsely chop one onion and finely slice the other. Chop the ginger, the garlic and the chilli. Grind 2 tsp of the cumin seeds and cut the pork into bite sized chunks.

Put the onion, the chilli, and half each of the ginger and garlic, together with the lentils, ground cumin and tumeric, into a pan with about a pint of water. Bring to the boil, cover, and simmer very gently for 30-40 minutes. You may need a little more water.

Add the pork and salt to the mixture; simmer for another 20-30 minutes until the meat is just cooked and the rest should be a thick mush.

Meanwhile put a little oil in a small pan on a medium heat; add the 1tsp of whole cumin seeds and sizzle for a few seconds. Add the remaining ginger and garlic and fry for a few minutes until the garlic is browning. Stir in the cayenne. Tip it all into the pan with the pork and lentils.

Now add the lemon juice, sugar and garam masala. Stir and simmer for another few minutes. Sprinkle with coriander leaves and serve with rice, bulgur or couscous.

TIPS AND VARIATIONS-

- chicken or lamb pieces are a good substitute for pork
- you could add a few frozen peas or green beans when putting in the lemon juice
- keeps and reheats very well
- to make your own garam masala - see page 189.

BROWN LENTILS WITH ONION AND GARLIC

Lentils have the advantage over most pulses that they do not need soaking before cooking. This simple dish is a great accompaniment to any Indian meal, an easy vegetarian option, and a good alternative to rice or couscous or bulgar

250g brown lentils

medium onion

3 cloves garlic

2tsps whole cumin seeds

sunflower oil

1tsp salt

½tsp cayenne pepper

NOTES

Peel and coarsely chop the onion. Finely chop the garlic.

In a large heavy pan over a medium hot heat fry the cumin seeds in a little oil for a few seconds. Add the garlic and stir around briefly; then add the onion, stir frying until they are starting to brown, just a few minutes.

Add the lentils, stir around and put in enough water to rather more than cover. Bring to the boil, cover, lower the heat and simmer gently for 30-40 minutes.

The lentils should end up tender and the mixture thick and nearly dry. Towards the end remove the lid or add more water as necessary – put in the salt and cayenne near the end of the cooking time.

Tips and Variations-

- add some other spices to jazz it up a little
- quite pleasant warm or cold and improves with reheating
- near the end of cooking add some diced vegetables, eg french beans, carrots or peas

CAULIFLOWER FLORETS

An appetizing hors d'oeuvre in its own right, hot or cold, but also a very
tasty vegetable accompaniment to grills, roasts and many curry dishes.

a medium head of cauliflower

6tbs sunflower oil

1tbs black mustard seeds

½ tbs fennel seeds

2 cloves garlic

½tsp tumeric

pinch of cayenne pepper

1tsp salt

NOTES

Cut all the florets from the cauliflower to 1 or 2 inches in size, and the tender parts of the stalks into smaller pieces; put to soak for 20 minutes in a bowl of cold water. Chop the garlic very finely.

Put the oil in a wok over a highish heat and stir in the mustard and fennel seeds for a few minutes until they start to 'pop'. Add the garlic for a few moments until lightly browned then stir in the tumeric and cayenne. Lower the heat.

Add the drained cauliflower florets, salt and 4tbs water. Stir around and cook over a medium heat for 10 minutes or so until the florets are just done.

They should retain some crispness and the water be all evaporated. You may need to cover the wok for a while to get them cooked through or possibly add more water if it evaporates too soon.

TIPS AND VARIATIONS-
- one of those dishes where you can vary the spices as to what is available
- try with courgettes instead of cauliflower

CURRIED CAULIFLOWER PILAFF

*A very good vegetarian dish, a vegetable accompaniment
or, cold, as part of a mixed hors d'oeuvre*

a small cauliflower

2 small red onions

150g basmati rice

2tbs medium curry paste

1tbs sunflower oil

2 tbs almonds

fresh coriander leaves

plain yoghurt

NOTES

Cut the cauliflower into small florets. Thinly slice one onion and finely chop the other. Lightly crush the almonds and coarsely chop the coriander leaves.

Put the oil in a large pan or wok with the onions and gently cook for a few minutes until softening. Add the rice and curry paste and stir around until the grains are well coated.

Pour in 500ml boiling water and add the cauliflower florets. Stir around, bring back to the boil, cover and simmer gently for 15 minutes or so until the rice is just tender, the liquid absorbed and the florets are just *al dente*. With luck all this will happen at the same time!

Stir in the crushed almonds and the coriander and serve with yoghurt.

TIPS AND VARIATIONS-

- you could try this using butternut squash instead of the cauliflower
- make your own curry paste
- sprinkle over a little garam masala just before serving

LAMB CURRY

An aromatic and easily made curry which benefits from a
good marinating time and seriously improves if reheated.

500g boned leg of lamb
2 large onions
2 walnut sized pieces of ginger
3 garlic cloves
1tbs coriander seeds
2tsp cumin seeds
1tsp cardamom pods
pinch of salt and cayenne
2tbs oil
1tbs tomato purée
100g thick plain yoghurt – greek style

NOTES

Cube the lamb into bite size chunks. Slice one onion and chop the other. Grate the ginger and chop the garlic. In a spice grinder, grind the coriander, cumin and cardamom to a powder.

In a food processor put the chopped onion, garlic, ginger, the ground spices and seasoning and liquidise to a smooth paste. Coat the lamb thoroughly with this mixture and refrigerate for at least one hour.

Heat the oil in a large pan, a wok is ideal, and cook the sliced onion until softened. Add the lamb mixture and stir well over a high heat for 5-10 minutes until the lamb is sealed and any liquid has evaporated.

Reduce the heat and stir in the tomato *purée* and half the yoghurt. Simmer for another 10 minutes or so until almost dry.

Stir in the rest of the yoghurt, cover and simmer very gently for 30 minutes stirring, occasionally until the meat is tender.

TIPS AND VARIATIONS-

- a lean leg is best – you don't really want any fatty bits
- use ready ground spices if you don't have a grinder

MERGUEZ SAUSAGES or BURGERS

*Merguez are the deliciously spicy red lamb sausages of North Africa, a Moroccan classic,
but just as good made as burgers if you don't happen to have sausage making machine!*

500g minced lamb

lemon

3 garlic cloves

2 tsps harissa

1 tsp ground cumin

½ tsp paprika

handful of fresh mint and coriander
leaves

NOTES

Grate the rind from the lemon. Finely chop the garlic, mint and coriander leaves.

Mix everything well together in a large bowl and chill for several hours to let the flavours develop.

If you do have a sausage making machine use that to make your sausages. Otherwise, by hand, squeeze the mixture into six or eight little patties, rather smaller than beef burgers.

Fry them in a little oil for a few minutes on each side until cooked through.

Serve with a couscous salad.

TIPS AND VARIATIONS-

- harissa is a hot spicy paste, based on chillies, garlic and tomato and used a lot in North Africa; it is available in most deli's
- shoulder of lamb is best for this as you need the fat
- these will do well on a barbeque

MINCED PORK CURRY

Quickly and easily made and, as with many curry dishes, improves with reheating

500g minced lean pork   NOTES
medium onion
3 garlic cloves
2tbs curry paste
125g dried apricots
large red pepper
seasoning
fresh coriander

Thinly slice the onion. Crush the garlic cloves with a little salt. Coarsely chop the apricots. Cut the peppers into thin strips.

In a non stick pan dry stir fry the mince for a few minutes until it changes colour. Add the onion and crushed garlic and cook for a few minutes longer.

Stir in the curry paste, apricots and pepper strip, together with a little water. Simmer, covered, for 10-12 minutes, then uncovered, for a few minutes more, until all the liquid has dried out.

Sprinkle with chopped coriander and serve with rice.

Tips and Variations–

- the cheaper cuts of pork are better; ask your butcher mince the meat if you don't have a mincer
- make your own curry paste by liquidising onion, garlic and ginger and adding ground cumin and coriander – or experiment with different spices
- if you don't have a non stick pan use just a minimum of oil

PERSIAN LAMB POLO

This is a great dish for a larger party, as it does not do so well in smaller amounts;
the preparation is simple and can largely be done beforehand and
it only really needs a salad to accompany

500g basmati rice

NOTES

1kg lean lamb

3-4 medium onions

250g dried apricots

125g seedless raisins

1tsp turmeric

2tsps ground cinnamon

sunflower oil

seasoning

Chop the lamb into bite sized chunks. Slice half the onions and chop the remainder.

In a large *sauté* pan soften all the onions in a little oil; add the lamb and quickly brown/seal over a higher heat; this may need to be done in two or more batches.

Season with salt and pepper, add the raisins, the apricots and the cinnamon and turmeric. Cover with water, just, and simmer very gently, covered, for 1-1½ hours until the meat is just tender. Uncover towards the end to ensure that most of the liquid has evaporated.

Meanwhile parboil the rice by cooking, uncovered, in boiling salted water for 8-10 minutes until nearly done. Strain, rinse in warm water and drain.

Warm a large casserole - which will be the serving dish - cover the bottom with a little oil. Put in a third of the parboiled rice, then half the lamb mixture, then another third of rice, the remaining lamb and finish with the rest of the rice.

Cover the casserole with a cloth and put on a low heat for 30 minutes or so.

TIPS AND VARIATIONS-
* cheaper cuts of lamb are best
* soaking the rice in salted water for several hours, or overnight, beforehand is traditional and makes it fluffier, but no matter if not
* it may be easier to brown the lamb by itself, then add back to the onions
* the cloth absorbs the steam and helps to make the rice lighter

SAUSAGE JAMBALAYA

A simple and spicy dish for a casual supper which can be made well in advance

500g sausages
2 medium onions
225g risotto rice (arborio)
2 cloves garlic
1tsp chilli powder
2tsp ground turmeric
olive oil
400ml stock
tin of chopped tomatoes
seasoning
a large courgette
red pepper
5-6 small mushrooms

NOTES

Divide each sausage into two and separate. Slice the onions and crush the garlic. Chop the pepper, slice the courgette and halve the mushrooms.

In a large pan, or wok, brown the sausages in some oil and then add the onions, chilli powder, turmeric, garlic and rice. Stirring gently, cook for 5-10 minutes until the rice goes opaque.

Add the stock, tomatoes and seasoning. Bring to the boil and simmer, covered, for 15-20 minutes.

Then add the courgettes, peppers and mushrooms and cook, uncovered, for 10-15 minutes or until all the liquid is absorbed. Keep warm until ready to serve.

TIPS AND VARIATIONS-

- use good quality sausages – smoked are traditional
- Jambalaya is really a Creole version of Spanish paella to which you can add anything suitable that is available
- add more spices or chopped chillies if you like a stronger flavour

SPICY AUBERGINE PIECES

*A tasty little nibble, quick and easy to make, and useful as an
hors d'oeuvre or accompaniment to a roast or an Indian style meal*

large aubergine
1tsp salt
1tsp black pepper
½tsp turmeric
1tsp ground cumin
½tsp cayenne pepper
sunflower oil
1 lemon

NOTES

Halve the aubergine lengthways and then cut across, on an angle, into ½" slices. Lay them out on a chopping board. Cut the lemon into 6 or 8 wedges.

Mix well together in a small bowl the salt, turmeric, cumin, black and cayenne pepper. Sprinkle half of this mixture generously over the aubergine slices.

Over a medium heat put a large frying pan with 2 to 3 tbs of oil. When hot add the aubergine slices, spicy side down, in a single layer. Fry until reddish brown on the underside. This will only take a few minutes.

Sprinkle over the remaining spice mixture, turn the slices over and fry similarly. Remove and serve, on their own, with the lemon wedges.

TIPS AND VARIATIONS-
- if you find any of the baby aubergines sold in Indian delicatessens, these are especially delicious
- if you think they are going to be too spicy, cover one side only
- if there is a surplus of oil on the pieces, drain them on kitchen paper
- alternatively, cook on a baking tray, without oil, in a medium hot oven

SPICY TUNA WITH PASTA

*A quick and simple but rather special dish which can easily be made
with ingredients from the store cupboard and usually to hand*

pasta shells   NOTES

olive oil

2 medium onions

green pepper

125g french beans

several garlic cloves

small fresh red chilli

1tsp cumin seed

seasoning

tin chopped tomatoes

standard tin of tuna

Slice all the vegetables, crush the garlic and finely chop the chilli. Drain the tuna.

Put a little oil in a large wok and briefly stir fry the vegetables.

Add the crushed garlic and cumin, chilli, tomatoes and seasoning. Cover and simmer for some ten
minutes. Add the tuna and warm through gently to amalgamate the flavours.

Meanwhile cook the pasta shells in fast boiling salted water until just *al dente*.

Toss everything together and serve.

TIPS AND VARIATIONS-
* vary cooking time as to whether you like vegetables well done or crisp
* experiment with added herbs, eg. coriander etc
* using fresh tomatoes and fresh tuna raise the level and quality no end
* instead of pasta shells, try serving on a bed of prepared couscous

AL
FRESCO

A colourful Bean Salad
Aubergine sweet and sour
Butterflied Leg of Lamb
Chicken Thonnata
Leek and smoked salmon salad
Minced lamb kebabs
Quinoan tabbouleh with feta
Ribbon Omelette Gateâu
Salad Niçoise
Two simple Beetroot Salads

A MEAL OUT OF doors and the food always seems so much more vibrant and tasty. Why should this be? Whether a barbeque, a picnic out in the countryside, supper on the patio or a lunch on the lawn under the trees, invariably there is that extra 'zing' to everything.

The risk of rain with a sudden dash for cover has an element of adventure. The fresh air alone adds atmosphere to the ambience. It is romantic, even exciting. But most of all its probably because, in this country at least, we just don't do it very often. So take a chance and go for it, but do be practical and always have a fall back position!

You can of course make a meal of pretty well anything outside; but some dishes do seem much more appropriate and these few recipes I have found lend themselves particularly well. Barbequeing can be very labour intensive, all that turning and shifting bits around; but this butterflied leg of lamb will feed 8-10 comfortably with a minimum of effort. I am especially proud of the ribbon omelette gateau, a recipe I came across very many years ago, and have made every year since for our annual family picnic down on the banks of the river Teme. But I have never seen, nor heard of it, anywhere else.

But most importantly - when entertaining do make sure that you give yourself plenty of time to enjoy the company of your friends.

A COLOURFUL BEAN SALAD

Dried beans are particularly good in salads as their rather bland flavour
contrasts well with crunchy vegetables and a strong sharp french dressing

125g flageolet beans   NOTES
125g red kidney beans
125g chick peas
2 shallots or 6 spring onions
5tbs french dressing with mustard
green pepper
red pepper
handful of mixed herbs
seasoning

Prepare the beans separately. Soak them overnight in water, drain and then simmer in salted fresh water until just tender. The chick peas can take some time.

Drain well and mix with the dressing in a serving dish.

Meanwhile finely chop the shallots or onions, deseed and slice the peppers and chop the herbs.

Season well and toss all together.

TIPS AND VARIATIONS-
- using tinned beans saves a lot of time as they need no soaking or cooking
- make double the quantity of chick peas and use the rest for hoummus
- these beans make a good contrast, but use others such as haricot or black eyed
- will keep well in the fridge for several days
- the dressing should be fairly thick
- reserve the cooking liquor from the chick peas and use a little in the dressing

AUBERGINE SWEET AND SOUR

*Delicious hot, cold or anywhere in between - goes well with
roast lamb or cold as part of a mixed hors d'oeuvre*

1 large aubergine

2-3tbs sunflower oil

3tbs balsamic vinegar

2tsps sugar

large pinch salt

bunch of spring onions

½tsp chilli powder

NOTES

Cut the aubergine into 1" chunks and finely slice the spring onions - long ways.

In a wide pan or wok heat the oil until smoking hot and then quickly fry the aubergine pieces until cooked and well browned, about 5-8 minutes. Drain on absorbent kitchen roll.

Put the balsamic vinegar, salt and sugar in the pan (remove any remaining oil) and simmer with the spring onions and chilli for a few minutes. Replace the aubergines; stir all together for a few more minutes and then serve.

TIPS AND VARIATIONS-

* instead of chilli powder use finely chopped red chilli or crushed dried chillies
* this is a great barbeque accompaniment
* use garlic instead of chilli

'BUTTERFLIED' LEG OF LAMB

A favourite barbeque dish - because of the varying thickness of the lamb
you get some well done and crispy bits as well as lots of pink and in between bits

leg of lamb

4-5 cloves of garlic

fresh rosemary

NOTES

Ask your butcher to 'butterfly' the lamb. This involves cutting the bone out of the leg and arranging the meat in an extended flat shape which vaguely resembles a butterfly. It is easily done oneself, which is more satisfying.

Cut the cloves of garlic into thin slithers and insert, with a rosemary leaf, into little slits cut into the fat and meat of the lamb. How much of this you do is a matter of taste and time, but the more the better. Roll up the leg and keep in the fridge until ready.

Cook over a hot barbeque grill for about 25-30 minutes each side. Carve into thickish slices.

TIPS AND VARIATIONS-

- shoulder of lamb is just as good, though fattier and more tricky to bone
- cook a few sausages at the same time
- this can of course be cooked in the oven or under a grill – not so good
- cook the lean side first – this means the fat on top has dried out a bit and is less likely to flare up when turned over
- an alternative is to marinate the butterflied lamb for several hours, or overnight, in a mixture of spices
- tomato *provéncale* – see page 168 - goes very well with this
- slice courgettes or aubergines lengthwise and barbeque at the same time

CHICKEN THONNATA

A wonderful dish for a cold buffet table or outside in the summer sunshine
the elegant combination of the different piquant tastes is intriguing

3-4 skinless chicken breasts

2 medium onions

2 sticks celery

2 bay leaves

sea salt and peppercorns

small tin of tuna (in oil)

4 anchovy fillets

juice of ½ lemon

1 tsp horseradish sauce

1 tbs capers

3-4 tbs mayonnaise

parsley

NOTES

Coarsely chop the onion and the celery. Drain the oil from the tuna tin.

Poach the chicken breasts by placing in cold water, covered, and bringing slowly to the boil. Skim off any froth, add the onion, celery, seasoning and bay leaves and simmer for 15 minutes.

Remove from the heat and leave to cool in the stock for 20 minutes. Remove the breasts which should be just cooked. Drain and reserve the stock, discarding the vegetable bits.

Put the drained tuna, anchovies, lemon juice, horseradish and capers with 3 tablespoons of the reserved stock into a blender and whiz into a *purée*. Stir in enough of the mayonnaise to give a thick coating sauce. Refrigerate until you are ready to serve.

Slice the breasts thickly and arrange on a serving platter. Coat with the thonnata sauce. Decorate with chopped parsley and a few capers.

TIPS AND VARIATIONS-

- serve with a salad of lettuce hearts and couscous
- this also works well with veal
- an excellent alternative to the ubiquitous coronation chicken

LEEK AND SMOKED SALMON SALAD

*This warm salad is very useful if you grow your own leeks and
need a use for the thinnings when planting out in late summer*

350g thin young leeks
125g oyster mushrooms
250g smoked salmon
2 little gem lettuces
olive oil
black pepper
black olives
lemon juice

NOTES

Clean the leeks and slice longways. Tear the mushrooms into wedges. Cut the salmon into strips. Cut the little gems lengthwise into wedge shaped sections.

Heat the oil in a pan and over a medium heat cook the leeks until almost tender. Add the mushroom pieces and continue cooking until just done.

Meanwhile arrange the lettuce onto serving plates.

Add the salmon to the pan with the leeks and mushroom, just for a few moments, toss around and then arrange over the lettuce.

Pour over any remaining pan juices, season with pepper and lemon juice and garnish with the black olives.

TIPS AND VARIATIONS-
- try with hot smoked salmon
- you could use older leeks; they'll just need to cook a little longer
- any old mushrooms can be an alternative

MINCED LAMB KEBABS

An ideal barbeque dish, delicately aromatic rather than spicy

500g minced lamb

3tbs split red lentils

1tsp cloves

1tsp green cardamom seeds

½tsp peppercorns

½tsp fennel seeds

1tsp cumin seeds

2 garlic cloves

1 medium red onion

1 medium red chilli

1 lime

1 egg

oil and seasoning

NOTES

In a small pan dry roast the lentils, cloves, cardamom, peppercorns, fennel and cumin for a few minutes until lightly browned and aromatic. Then grind them to a powder.

Finely chop the onion and *sauté* in a little oil until soft. Finely chop the garlic and deseeded chilli and grate the rind from the lime. Beat the egg.

Put the lamb in a mixing bowl and add the spice mixture, garlic, onion, chilli, lime zest and season to taste. Stir well together and add enough egg to give a binding mixture.

Divide the mixture into 5 or 6 portions and by hand wrap around wooden skewers so as to form a large sausage. Grill for 10-15 minutes on the barbeque turning occasionally.

Serve with lime or lemon wedges, yoghurt with chopped mint or coriander, or tzatziki – see page 43.

TIPS AND VARIATIONS-

- it is probably best to use leg meat as it does not want to be too fatty
- soak the wooden skewers beforehand for 30 minutes, so they do not burn
- instead of the lentils you could use split peas or chick peas – the idea is to add a slightly floury texture
- you could of course cook under a grill or on a griddle
- there are very many variations on this recipe using different spices and chopped herbs – so have fun, experiment and note the different tastes
- you could form them into burgers and cook like that

QUINOAN TABBOULEH WITH FETA

Quinoa is a relatively little known grain from South America where it was cultivated by the Incas for thousands of years. It has a delicate nutty flavour and is an excellent substitute for rice or bulgar in many dishes

250g quinoa

medium red onion

5-6 cherry tomatoes

2 large courgettes

½ cucumber

handful of parsley

6-8 mint leaves

250g feta cheese

olive oil and lemon juice

seasoning

Boil the quinoa, uncovered, in twice its volume of water for about 15 minutes. Cover and let it cool, when it will have doubled or more in volume. Drain.

Cut the courgettes lengthwise into thin strips. Brush with oil and cook on a hot griddle pan or barbeque for 5-6 minutes each side. Allow to cool on kitchen paper.

Meanwhile, halve and very thinly slice the onion. Halve or quarter the tomatoes. Cut the cucumber into chunks. Coarsely chop the parsley and mint. Cut the feta into small cubes. Make a dressing with the oil and lemon juice.

In a large bowl combine the quinoa, onion, tomatoes, cucumber and herbs. Just before serving gently stir in enough dressing to coat lightly. Then mix in the feta and courgette strips.

TIPS AND VARIATIONS-

- quinoa is not so easily available but can be found in most health food shops
- intensify its flavour by dry roasting the quinoa for a few minutes first

RIBBON OMELETTE GÂTEAU

Very time consuming to make- and it should be done the day before- but well worth the effort, this original and exotically beautiful dish is brilliant at any 'al fresco' meal or picnic

16 free range eggs

4 tbs tomato purée

500g spinach

sea salt and fresh ground pepper

a little thyme and a few chopped chives

150g emmental or cheddar cheese

flour, butter and milk

cayenne pepper

6-8 thin slices ham

dijon mustard

NOTES

The *gâteau* is made by stacking up alternate layers of tomato and spinach omelettes interspersed with ham and cheese. When unwrapped it does not look much, but when cut into wedges, like a cake, all its glory is revealed.

For the golden tomato omelettes; whisk up 8 eggs with the tomato *purée* very thoroughly (or liquidise). Add salt, pepper and thyme. Make 6-8 very thin omelettes, cooked on one side only – like making pancakes but without turning – and reserve.

For the green omelettes; cook the spinach in a little boiling salted water, cool, drain and squeeze dry. Chop. Whisk up with the remaining 8 eggs, chives and a pinch of salt. Make another 6-8 very thin omelettes, again without turning them over – and reserve.

Grate the cheese and with the flour, butter and milk make a cheese sauce in the usual way, but rather on the thick side. Stir in a pinch of cayenne and let it cool.

Put a spinach omelette, cooked side down, on a sheet of foil. Spread it sparingly with the cheese sauce. Put a tomato omelette on top, cooked side up. Spread lightly with the mustard and put on a layer of ham with another thin spread of mustard on top to make it sticky. Add another spinach omelette cooked side down and continue with alternating layers until all are used up.

Wrap the stack lightly in foil, press gently together and chill overnight. Serve on a round board and cut with a very sharp knife.

Tips and Variations-

- a little hot water with the tomato *purée* helps it amalgamate with the eggs
- these quantities will do 15-20 as a starter, but adding more of everything with extra layers to the stack makes the *gâteau* look even more impressive when cut
- a 7"- 8" omelette pan is best – larger and you won't have enough omelettes
- allow a good 2-3 hours to make and construct your *gâteau*

SALAD NIÇOISE

A classic summer lunch-time dish with many possible variations

250g tuna – fresh or canned   NOTES
2 little gem lettuces
250g french beans
500g ripe tomatoes
350g new potatoes
bunch of spring onions
½ tin anchovy fillets
2 eggs
black olives
garlic
french dressing

There is quite a lot of preparation involved in this recipe and the presentation is all important.

If using fresh tuna, grill or fry, till just done and flake into pieces. Quarter the lettuces and simmer the french beans in salted water until just *al dente*. Skin the tomatoes and cut into quarters. Cook the potatoes- preferably with a little mint- until just done, and cut into walnut sized pieces. Slice the spring onions longways. Hard boil the eggs, peel and quarter.

The salad is best presented on a large dish as a whole, but can be done on individual plates.

Rub the garlic over the dish and spread over the lettuce leaves. Toss the beans, tomatoes and potatoes lightly in the french dressing and arrange over the lettuce with the eggs. Pile the tuna in the centre of the dish with the anchovies crossed over. Scatter the spring onions and olives over the whole.

TIPS AND VARIATIONS-

- tinned tuna is fine, but fresh is a great deal better
- serve while the tuna is still warm
- good quality ingredients are all important
- add a few chopped fresh herbs
- crumble the yolk from one of the egg quarters and scatter over the salad

TWO SIMPLE BEETROOT SALADS

Beetroot has quite a strong, but sweet and earthy, flavour which does not suit everyone.
To me its distinctive taste is quite delicious. It is also good hot as a vegetable accompaniment, but
these two salads make an excellent starter on their own or as a part of a mixed hors d'oeuvres

500g cooked beetroot   NOTES

100g shallot or onion

3tbs olive oil

1tbs lemon juice

seasoning and brown sugar to taste

chopped chives, parsley or coriander

Finely chop the shallot, slice or cube the beetroot and put together in a bowl.

Make a dressing by whisking together the oil, lemon juice, seasoning and sugar to taste.

Mix all together and serve garnished with the herbs.

6-8 cooked beetroots   NOTES

2 large oranges

4tbs olive oil

1½ tbs lemon juice

1tsp made mustard

salt, pepper and sugar to taste

Peel the oranges and slice thickly – cut the beetroot into rounds. Arrange the slices alternately overlapping in a shallow dish.

Whisk together all the dressing ingredients and spoon over the salad just before serving.

TIPS AND VARIATIONS-

- boil raw beetroot for 60-90 minutes until just tender and rub off the skin
- both these salads will keep well if made some hours before eating
- smaller beetroot are more tasty and succulent
- serve the orange beetroot salad on a bed of watercress
- grate the orange peel and add some to the dressing

VEGETABLES

Alternative runner beans
Beetroot curry
Carrot and swede bake
Cucumber ragout
Cumin flavoured carrots, peas and
     potatoes
Fennel gratin
Aïgroissade
Leeks à la Grècque
Pommes gratin
Red pepper and garlic compote
Roasted ratatouille
Spinach with lentils and Catalan
     spinach
Spring green mallum
Tomatoes Provénçal

I LOVE MY VEGETABLE garden and the very simple pleasure of planting the seeds, cultivating, observing as they grow, then the satisfaction of harvesting, cooking and eating straight from the garden.

The quality of vegetables depends much both on the quality of soil in which they are grown, and the degree of care bestowed on their culture; but if produced in ever so great perfection, their excellence will be entirely destroyed if they be badly cooked. 'Modern Cookery for Private Families', Eliza Acton 1845.

'Overcooking and keeping hot' are the two quickest ways to ruin vegetables, say the French, and how right they are.

One should start with the idea that all vegetables can be treated as luxuries, not just asparagus and other such exotica, but even the ubiquitous cabbage and potato; for example turnips as in *navettes glacées* are absolutely wonderful. But the pre-eminent quality of all, when well treated, is that of delicacy.

It used to be a case of a meat and two veg; nowadays its very often four or five veg, which is just too many. One, or perhaps two, interestingly prepared vegetable dishes will be a much better complement to an attractive main meal.

There are so many marvellous things to be done with vegetables; substantial, delicate and decorative, that the thought of being a vegetarian would give me very few qualms.

This small, but varied, selection gives, I hope, an idea of the potential and the possibilities. Some of these could be served as a first course.

ALTERNATIVE RUNNER BEANS

Whilst normally boiled or steamed, this is an attractive recipe that gives a bit more interest to the beans – unlike French beans there are not so many recipes using runners

400g runner beans   NOTES
2 medium spring onions
2 rashers streaky bacon
butter
seasoning
handful oregano

Top and tail the beans and cut off the stringy bit down the sides. Coarsely chop into 1" pieces. Chop the onions and the bacon into similar sized bits. Chop the oregano.

In a little butter slowly cook the bacon and onion until softened.

Add the runner beans and seasoning; cover and simmer very gently over a low heat, stirring occasionally, for 20 minutes or so until the beans are just cooked.

Stir in the chopped oregano half way through, saving a little to garnish.

TIPS AND VARIATIONS-
- when seasoning remember the bacon will be salty
- use parsley, coriander or other fresh green herbs if necessary
- goes well with roast meat and grills

BEETROOT CURRY

This might seem an unusual idea for a vegetable curry but the natural sweetness
of the beetroot goes really well with the fragrant spices and the colour is magnifique

3-4 medium size beetroot, raw

1 medium onion

½ a tin of chopped tomatoes

2 good garlic cloves

a green chilli

bay leaf

1tsp turmeric

1½ tsps whole cumin seeds

½ a cinnamon stick

juice of half a lemon

125ml coconut milk

2tbs sunflower oil

1tsp whole mustard seeds

NOTES

Peel the beetroot and cut into *julienne* strips. Finely chop the onion and garlic. Deseed and cut the chilli into thin strips.

Put the oil into a wok, or a large pan, over a medium heat. Add the mustard seeds and in a minute or two, when they start to jump around, add the onion, garlic and chilli. Cook for 10 minutes or so until the onion is softening.

Increase the heat slightly and add the beetroot, bay leaf, turmeric, cinnamon and cumin. Stir fry for a few minutes. Add the tomato, a little water and a pinch of salt. Cover, lower the heat and simmer gently for 20-25 minutes until the beetroot is just cooked.

Then stir in the coconut milk and cook uncovered for some minutes until thickening. Add the lemon juice and serve.

TIPS AND VARIATIONS-

- a mandolin will cut up the beetroot in a trice
- reheats well and keeps for a few days in the fridge
- you could add some ground spices with the coconut milk, eg garam masala

CARROT AND SWEDE BAKE

This is Liz's lovely mellow vegetable accompaniment, a great vegetarian dish in its own right and it can be prepared well in advance

750g swede

500g carrots

butter

3tbs orange juice

125ml double cream

seasoning

2 slices dry brown bread

75g oatmeal

100g cheddar cheese

parsley

NOTES

Grate the swede and the carrots. Chop the parsley and grate the cheese. Process the bread into crumbs.

Stir fry the grated swede and carrot in butter for 10-15 minutes until beginning to soften. Stir in the orange juice and cream. Season well and put in a shallow serving dish.

For the topping, gently fry the breadcrumbs and oatmeal in butter until crisp. Cool. Stir in some chopped parsley and the grated cheese.

Cover the carrot and swede mixture with the topping and bake in a medium oven for 25 minutes or so until nicely browned on top.

TIPS AND VARIATIONS-

- none of the quantities need be very precise
- use fresh orange juice
- try with parsnips in place of swede
- not bad cold and reheats well
- this recipe comes from my friend Liz who is a top cook

CUCUMBER RAGOÛT

Too many cucumbers all at once in the greenhouse?
Try this simple vegetable accompaniment

2 cucumbers

2 medium onions

butter

5tbs chicken stock

3tbs dry white wine

1dsp flour

seasoning

Thinly slice the onions. Deseed the cucumbers and cut into 1" chunks – leave the skin on unless it is coarse or you prefer without.

Fry the onions in a little butter for a few minutes. Remove and quickly brown the cucumber pieces in the remaining butter.

Put both in a pan with the stock, wine and seasoning to taste. Cover and simmer very gently for 10-15 minutes or so until just cooked.

Mash the flour and softened butter together to make a *beurre manié*. Add a little of the liquid and stir back into the *ragoût*, little by little, until the sauce is fairly thick.

Check seasoning. Serve as a vegetable accompaniment.

Tips and Variations-

* this goes well with roast chicken or fried fish
* stock cubes are fine but its always better, and so easy, to make your own
* take care not to overcook – the cucumber chunks need to remain whole with a little bite, not reduced to a mush
* cheat and use sauce thickening granules!

CUMIN FLAVOURED CARROTS, PEAS AND POTATOES

*This spicy vegetable dish, with its many variations, goes well with roasts
or grills, or with most curry dishes, but also makes a very nice starter*

200g carrots

200g potatoes

200g onions

200g frozen peas

3tbs sunflower oil

2tsp cumin seeds

1tsp mustard seeds

2 small dried red chillies

1tsp salt

½ tsp sugar

4 spring onions

NOTES

Cut the carrots and potatoes into a ½" dice. Coarsely chop the onions. Thinly slice the spring onions lengthways.

Put the oil in a large wok or heavy pan and, over a medium heat, fry the cumin and mustard seeds with the chillies for half a minute, stirring. Add the chopped onion and stir around for 5-10 minutes until softening.

Stir in the carrots, cover, and cook for 5-10 minutes before adding the potatoes. Continue to cook until the vegetables are nearly tender. This may take a while.

Add the frozen peas, salt and sugar. Continue stirring; put in the spring onions a minute or two before serving.

TIPS AND VARIATIONS-

- remove the little chillies before serving
- try butternut squash instead of potatoes, broad or french beans in place of peas
- the vegetables all need to be just cooked through, rather than *'al dente'*, and the length of time involved is very much a matter of judgement
- sprinkle with ground coriander or garam masala just before serving

FENNEL GRATIN

*The roots of Florentine fennel have a delicate aniseed
flavour which goes especially well with gruyère cheese*

4 fennel bulbs

100g gruyère cheese

seasoning

butter

Halve the fennel bulbs, lengthwise, or quarter if large, and put into boiling salted water. Simmer until tender, about 30 minutes.

Grate the cheese. Drain the fennel and arrange in a greased baking dish. Sprinkle with seasoning and spread the grated *gruyère* on top.

Dot with butter and brown lightly under a grill or in a hot oven.

TIPS AND VARIATIONS-

* this can also make an attractive starter
* mix some breadcrumbs in with the grated cheese

AÏGROISSADE

This is a simple Provençal salad of spring vegetables dressed in a garlic mayonnaise, aïoli,

french beans

baby carrots

broad beans

young courgettes

chick peas

5-6 tbs aïoli

1 hard boiled egg and parsley

Soak the chick peas, drain, and simmer until cooked. Steam or boil the vegetables until just tender. Cut or slice them into evenly sized pieces.

Mix everything together in a serving dish and sprinkle over the chopped egg and parsley.

TIPS AND VARIATIONS-

* use about equal quantities of vegetables; you may already have some cooked chickpeas
* make aïoli by mixing together crushed garlic with mayonnaise

LEEKS À LA GRÈCQUE

Easily and quickly made, equally good hot or cold,
and a great way to use up surplus garden leeks

5-6 medium leeks   NOTES

medium onion

400g tin of chopped tomatoes

glass of white wine

5tbs olive oil

good pinch of dried mixed herbs

3 fat cloves garlic

sugar, salt and pepper

Clean the leeks, using only the white part, and cut into 1½" pieces. Chop the onion. Crush and chop the garlic.

Put all the ingredients into a heavy pan. Cover and simmer very gently, stirring from time to time, for 20-30 minutes, or longer, until the leeks are tender and the liquid reduced to a gooey consistency.

Serve hot as a vegetable accompaniment, or alternatively cold, as an *hors d'oeuvres*.

Tips and Variations-

- add 1-2tbs tomato *purée* to intensify the flavour, and less of the tomato
- you can parboil the leeks first to speed things up, but I think they lose flavour
- if necessary remove the leeks and reduce the residue on its own to get the right thick consistency
- keeps well in the fridge for several days
- works much better in a wide pan where the leeks can be spread in one layer

POMMES GRATIN

*There are many variations on the basic principle of this classically simple potato dish
Savoyard, Dauphinois, Lyonnaise and, when well done, all are delicious*

750g potatoes

250g onions

2 garlic cloves

125g gruyère cheese

butter

salt, pepper and grated nutmeg

250ml stock

NOTES

Peel and thinly slice the potatoes and the onions. Grate the cheese and crush and chop the garlic.

Mix butter and garlic to grease a shallow baking dish. Spread over in layers the potatoes, onions and cheese, sprinkling with seasonings and any remaining garlic. Finish with potatoes on top dotted with butter and cheese.

Pour in the stock to just below the last potato layer and cook in a medium hot oven for about 1 hour, until golden on top and all is cooked through.

TIPS AND VARIATIONS–

- goes particularly well with grills and roasts
- take care not to put in too much stock - it should end up moist but not runny
- cheddar or any hard cheese is good too
- try adding a layer of thinly sliced courgettes
- for *pommes Dauphinois* use cream and milk instead of stock and no cheese or onion
- *pommes Savoyarde* uses stock without cheese or onion
- *pommes Lyonnaise* is just thinly sliced potato and onion baked in butter or pork fat
- ***PITHIVIERS SAVOYARDE** – this is an excellent way to create individual dishes.* Make the gratin as above but cut the potato rather smaller. Divide the potato mixture into individual portions and put each onto a small square of rolled out short cut pastry. Fold the pastry around to form little parcels. Bake the parcels in a medium hot oven for 20-30 minutes until golden.

RED PEPPER AND GARLIC COMPÔTE

*This variation on a Delia Smith recipe is a delicious accompaniment
to grilled meats or a barbeque – an alternative to chutney*

6 red peppers

8-10 garlic cloves

3tbs olive oil

2 tsps cumin seed

4 tbs tomato purée

1tps cayenne pepper

salt

NOTES

Deseed the peppers and cut into strips, abt ¼" thick. Lightly crush the cumin seeds. Peel and finely chop the garlic.

Toss the cumin seed in a large pan over a medium heat for a few minutes – this draws out their flavour. Add the oil and stir around for a few moments.

Add the peppers, garlic and cayenne and stir around so all thoroughly mixed together. Cover the pan and cook gently on a low heat for 30-40 minutes or so until the pepper strips are quite soft.

Increase the heat to medium, stir in the tomato *purée*, and cook, uncovered, and keep stirring, until all the liquid is absorbed or evaporated – abt 10-15 minutes – it should be quite sticky. Taste and add a little salt or more tomato *purée* as appropriate.

Serve warm or cool, but not chilled.

TIPS AND VARIATIONS-

- you can use yellow or orange peppers, or a mix – but not green
- do not be frightened of this sort of dish because of the quantity of garlic – it loses all of it's pungency in the cooking leaving a delicate aroma
- keeps for a week or so in the fridge
- goes well with grills, roasts and a barbeque

ROASTED RATATOUILLE

Traditional ratatouille is a great Mediterranean dish but try this
'dry roasted' version as an attractive and easily made alternative

2 red peppers

1 aubergine

3 courgettes

8-10 small tomatoes

1 medium onion

3 fat garlic cloves

handful fresh herbs

olive oil

seasoning

NOTES

Deseed and slice the peppers. Cut the aubergine and courgettes into 1" chunks. Skin the tomatoes and halve if large. Slice the onion and chop the herbs. Finely chop the garlic.

Spread out all the vegetables in a large shallow roasting tin. Sprinkle over the garlic, herbs, and olive oil. Toss it all around so that all the vegetables are lightly coated with the oil. Add the seasoning.

Cook in a very hot oven for 40 minutes or so until the vegetables are softening and going brown round the edges. Serve at once.

TIPS AND VARIATIONS-

- salt and drain the aubergine if you wish, but I think it makes little difference
- include green or yellow peppers
- skin tomatoes by covering in boiling water for one minute; prick the skin which will then slip off
- use as a pancake filling with a cheese sauce for a light lunch dish

SPINACH

If you grow your own spinach there will be times when it seems impossible to keep up with it - here are two excellent ways to help, one Indian and one Spanish

BROWN LENTILS AND SPINACH

200g brown lentils

medium onion

4 cloves garlic

1tsp whole cumin seeds

4tbs sunflower oil

400g spinach

salt and cayenne pepper

NOTES

Peel and chop the garlic and the onion. Wash and coarsely chop the spinach and blanch for 2 minutes. Squeeze it dry.

In a large heavy pan fry the cumin seeds for a few seconds. Add the garlic and then the onion stir frying until they are starting to brown. Add the lentils and cover with water.

Cover and simmer gently for 30-40 minutes until only just moist and the lentils are cooked. Add the spinach and seasoning 10 minutes from finishing.

CATALAN SPINACH

500g spinach leaves

4-5 tbs sultanas

3 garlic cloves

medium onion

4 tbs pine nuts

2 tbs olive oil and seasoning

NOTES

Soak the sultanas in hot water for 15-20 minutes. Dry roast the pine nuts for a few minutes in a small pan. Roughly chop the spinach. Finely chop the onion and garlic.

Heat the oil in a large heavy pan and fry the onion, followed by the garlic, for a few minutes until the onion has softened. Add the spinach, stir around and cover. Cook for 5-10 minutes when the spinach should have wilted.

Add the drained sultanas, the pine nuts and seasoning. Stir around for a few more minutes until all is warmed through and serve at once.

TIPS AND VARIATIONS-
- you could soak the sultanas in sherry – but do not drain!
- the ingredients in these recipes can be very approximate

SPRING GREEN MALLUM

There are many delicious ways of cooking cabbages, other than the all too normal boiling, and this Sri Lankan spiced and stir fried dish is excellent

1 large spring cabbage
2tbs sunflower oil
1tsp mustard seeds
medium onion
1 green chilli
1tsp turmeric
1tsp salt
juice of half a lemon
3tsps desiccated coconut

NOTES

Slice the cabbage fairly thinly. Halve and thinly slice the onion. Deseed and finely chop the chilli.

Heat the oil in a wok until smoking hot, then add the mustard seeds. After a few moments, when they start to pop, put in the onion, cabbage and chilli. Stir fry for 4-5 minutes.

Add the turmeric, salt and coconut and continue stir frying for a few more minutes until the coconut starts to colour and the cabbage to soften.

Remove from the heat, stir in the lemon juice and serve.

TIPS AND VARIATIONS-
- you can use any sort of cabbage, although Savoy probably works best
- goes well with roast chicken, spicy curries and many other dishes
- 'mallum' basically means shredded green leaves

TOMATOES PROVÉNCALE

An attractive and easily made accompaniment to roast meat dishes which goes particularly well with a leg of lamb

4 large firm but ripe tomatoes

seasoning

2 large garlic cloves

handful of parsley

2 slices dry bread

4 tbs olive oil

NOTES

Process the bread into crumbs. Crush and chop the garlic cloves. Chop the parsley.

Cut the tomatoes in half horizontally and cut out a small depression in the centre. Sprinkle with salt and pepper.

In a bowl mix together the parsley, garlic and breadcrumbs. Add enough oil to moisten well.

Fill the tomatoes with the mixture and arrange in a shallow dish.

Bake for 15-20 minutes in a medium hot oven.

TIPS AND VARIATIONS-
- slice off a little of the tomato bottoms to make them stand up
- add the cut off tomato bits to the mixture
- make the breadcrumbs in a liquidizer, and just add the parsley and garlic whole
- this looks very pretty surrounding a joint of lamb or pork

PUDDINGS

Alternative mince tart
Beetroot and chocolate gâteau
Bread and butter pudding with rhubarb
Chocolate and cranberry roulade
Clafoutis
Delicious plum dessert
Mango sundae
Lebanese fruit salad
Lissanoure
Pears in red wine
Rhubarb and ginger sponge puddings
Rice pudding
Sorbets

I WAS NEVER REALLY very much of a pudding person; indeed I do remember that many years ago it was quite common to have a savoury course at the end of a meal. Probably my tooth has sweetened over the years and anyway I felt the need to try a few in order to complete this book.

The words 'pudding' and 'dessert' are nowadays virtually interchangeable, but historically a pudding was a concoction of savoury ingredients cooked in the skin of an animal's intestine. Survivors today would be black pudding, haggis or the french andouillette. Pudding is derived from the french word 'boudin' meaning a black or white pudding or sausage. Later it was realised that these mixtures could more practically be steamed or boiled in a cloth and then in a bowl – steak and kidney pudding. It was only in the later 19th century that puddings took on their modern 'sweet' form and the mass production of cakes, chocolate and jellies began.

Elaborate and delicate preparations by gourmet chefs can be a wonder to behold, but these few simple and practical recipes are good enough for cooking at home.

ALTERNATIVE MINCE TART

A delicious and easily made Christmas holiday treat
and a nice change from traditional mince pies

225g shortcrust pastry

50g butter

50g brown sugar

175g currants

50g chopped walnuts

2 eggs

100g icing sugar

1-2 lemons

NOTES

Roll out the pastry and line an 8" loose based flan tin. Chill for half an hour.

Prick the pastry case all over with a fork, cover with grease proof paper and fill with baking beans. Blind bake for 10 minutes in a medium oven, c.200°C, remove the beans and paper and bake for another 5 minutes until the pastry is dry.

In a small pan gently heat and mix together the butter, brown sugar, currants and walnuts stirring all the time until melted. When cooled a little spread the mixture evenly into the pastry case. Beat the eggs and spread them evenly over the top.

Return to the oven for 15-20 minutes and bake until set. Allow to cool in the tin.

Mix the icing sugar with enough lemon juice to just give a pouring consistency and then spread this over the top. Leave to set.

TIPS AND VARIATIONS-

- make in small pastry cases like mince pies
- you could try different mixtures for the mincemeat, but why bother, when this is so good

BEETROOT AND CHOCOLATE GÂTEAU

*On the face of it this is not an obvious combination but it works so well-
rich, dark and moist, and merely a hint of beetroot flavour – to be eaten with a fork!*

125g plain flour

2 tbs cocoa powder

1½ tsps baking powder

pinch of salt

140g caster sugar

1tsp vanilla extract

3 eggs

200ml sunflower oil

250g beetroot

125g strong dark chocolate

crème fraîche or double cream

NOTES

Cook the beetroot, cool and skin, then grate coarsely. Beat the eggs. Chop or break the chocolate into very small pieces. Mix them all well together with the vanilla and oil.

Sift the flour, cocoa powder, baking powder and salt into a large mixing bowl. Stir in the sugar. Fold in the beetroot mixture and stir gently until everything is incorporated.

Grease a 7" cake tin and line with greaseproof paper. Pour in the mixture.

Bake for 50-60 minutes in a medium hot oven, c.190°C, until a skewer comes out clean.

Turn out the *gâteau* and cool on a rack. Serve with lots of *crème fraîche* or cream.

TIPS AND VARIATIONS-
* use ready cooked beetroot for convenience
* cook in a square, rather than round, cake tin to make it easier to apportion
* for a stronger flavour, use some, or all, peeled and grated raw beetroot

BREAD AND BUTTER
PUDDING WITH RHUBARB

Rhubarb adds a delectable touch to this already perfect pudding

4-5 tender rhubarb stalks

300g castor sugar

juice of one orange

7-8 thick slices bread

butter

1 tbs sultanas

200ml thick cream

300ml milk

4 eggs

NOTES

Cut the rhubarb into 1" lengths. Soak the sultanas in hot water for 20 minutes and drain. Butter the bread and cut into triangular quarters.

Simmer the rhubarb with half of the sugar and the orange juice for 20-30 minutes. Start with it covered, then uncovered, stirring occasionally, until ending up with a fairly dry *purée*. Let it cool.

Arrange most of the bread triangles in overlapping layers in a greased baking dish. Scatter with the sultanas and spread the rhubarb over. Finish with a layer of the remaining bread.

Gently heat the milk and cream together until just simmering and immediately remove from the heat. In a mixer beat together the eggs and other half of the sugar for a few minutes until thickened. Gradually pour in the milk and cream mixture while continuing to beat.

Pour this mixture over the bread and let it absorb for half an hour or so. Put in a medium oven, c.180°C, and bake for 40-50 minutes until golden on top.

TIPS AND VARIATIONS-

- keep back a little rhubarb and dot on top before baking
- try this with *purées* of other tart fruit
- you may not need quite so much bread

CHOCOLATE AND CRANBERRY ROULADE

*The slightly tart flavour of fresh cranberries gives a refreshing
contrast to the rich chocolate sponge in this sumptuous roulade*

175g cranberries
1 orange
225g caster sugar
4 eggs
100g plain continental chocolate
150ml double cream, whipped
cocoa powder and icing sugar for dusting

NOTES

Grate the zest from the orange and squeeze out the juice. Simmer the cranberries, zest and juice in a covered pan for a few minutes until the berries are soft. Stir in half the sugar over a gentle heat until dissolved. Let cool.

Grease, and line with greaseproof paper, a 12"x8" Swiss roll tin.

Whisk the eggs and remaining sugar in a bowl, over a pan of hot water, until pale and creamy. In another bowl, melt the chocolate over a pan of hot water, and then gently fold into the egg mixture.

Pour the combined mixture into the tin and level. Cook in a medium hot oven, 200°C, for about 15 minutes until just set.

Place a sheet of greaseproof paper over a damp tea towel and dredge with icing sugar. Turn out the cake onto the paper. Carefully remove the paper from the top. Trim the edges and roll up with the other sheet of paper inside. Leave to cool.

Unroll the cake very carefully. Spread the cranberry mixture evenly over it leaving a 1" gap at one end. Spread the whipped cream on top. Roll it up and dust with the cocoa powder and icing sugar. Chill until ready to serve.

TIPS AND VARIATIONS-

- cranberries are only in season from October to December, so freeze some for use in the rest of the year
- this needs careful handling as it can easily all fall to pieces!

CLAFOUTIS

Originally from the Limousin this is a traditional french cherry pudding in batter

500g fresh black cherries

125ml milk

2 eggs

2tsps vanilla essence

5 tbs icing sugar

6 tbs plain flour

pinch of salt

Stone the cherries leaving them as whole as possible. Grease a medium sized shallow baking dish with butter. The *clafoutis* will be served from this dish, so it should be presentable!

Make a batter by blending together in a large mixing bowl the milk, eggs and vanilla essence, using a wire whisk, until the liquid is smooth. Next add four tablespoons of the sugar, one by one, whisking all the time and then the flour similarly, finally the salt. You should end up with a very smooth and light pancake batter.

Pour the batter into the baking dish and spread the cherries evenly throughout it. Bake in a medium oven, c.180 °C, for 50-60 minutes.

Sprinkle the *clafoutis* with the remaining sugar and serve straight away with whipped cream, custard or *crème fraîche*.

TIPS AND VARIATIONS-

- you could do this with any other soft fruit in season, when it is known as a *flaugnarde* – try figs or blueberries
- much easier to buy a tin of ready stoned cherries!
- you are supposed to sift the flour but I'm not sure it makes any difference
- a useful test of when it is ready to come out of the oven is to insert a knife into the *clafoutis* which should come out clean when ready

DELICIOUS PLUM DESSERT

Simplicity itself and a perfect pudding

4 very large plums

65g unsalted butter

65g castor sugar

65g demerara sugar

65g icing sugar

sprig of thyme

3tbs brandy

Grease an ovenproof dish. Halve the plums, take out the stones and put face down in the dish. Finely chop the thyme leaves.

Soften the butter and mix well with the three sugars. It should be firm, not runny.

Place a knob of the sugar mixture on top of each plum and put the dish into a hot oven, c.250°C, for 15 minutes.

Spoon the brandy over the plums and scatter over the chopped thyme. Put back into the oven for 5 more minutes.

Serve with vanilla ice cream and a small ginger biscuit.

TIPS AND VARIATIONS-
- be more generous and double everything
- *crème fraîche* substitutes well for the ice cream

LEBANESE FRUIT SALAD

This is delicious and will mature nicely for 2-3 weeks in the fridge

250g dried stoned prunes

250g dried apricots

250g dried figs

jar of stem ginger

cinnamon stick

vanilla pod

2tbs dark brown sugar

50g pine nuts

2tbs orange juice

NOTES

Slice about 100g of the stem ginger and reserve 2tbs of the juice.

Put the dried fruits, ginger slices and juice, cinnamon and vanilla, and the sugar into a large pan. Add enough water to almost cover the fruits.

Cover the pan and bring to the boil. Simmer gently for 15-20 minutes, stirring occasionally. Check that the fruits are soft.

Allow to cool. Remove the cinnamon and vanilla. Stir in the nuts and orange juice.

Chill for several hours and serve with *crème fraîche* or cream.

TIPS AND VARIATIONS-
- use dried fruit that does not need soaking first
- you could use pistachio nuts
- adding the stem ginger pieces after simmering gives them a bit more bite
- use no more water than you need to or the liquid will be too thin
- try adding a little grated nutmeg or finely ground cloves

MANGO SUNDAE

A simple but rather pretty summer dessert of contrasting taste and colour

2 large ripe mangoes
150g raspberries
250g fromage frais

NOTES

Skin the mangoes and cut the flesh into ½" cubes. *Purée* the raspberries in a food processor.

Depending on how many portions are needed take 4-6 individual sundae glasses, or large wine glasses. First put some mango into the bottom of each glass. Then some *fromage frais*, followed by a layer of the raspberry *purée* and top with the remaining mangoes. Serve chilled.

TIPS AND VARIATIONS-

• use ice cream, yoghurt or *crème fraîche* instead of *fromage frais*
• there should be distinct layers – don't let it mix together

LISSANOURE

This is a traditional northern Irish recipe for a lemon tea cake

2 eggs
butter, weight equivalent to the eggs
sugar, ditto
flour, ditto
1 lemon
cupful of milk

NOTES

Separate the eggs. Grate the zest from the lemon and squeeze out the juice.

In a liquidiser, or food processor, mix well together everything except the egg whites.

Beat the egg whites with a whisk until stiff. Fold into the lemon mixture.

Put into a lightly buttered dish and bake in a *bain marie* in a medium hot oven, around 180°C, for 30-40 minutes. This magically separates into a lemon sauce with sponge on top when cooked. Eat hot with a little *crème fraîche.*

TIPS AND VARIATIONS-

• it helps to soften the butter first
• you could cook in 4-6 individual ramekins for a supper party

PEARS IN RED WINE

An attractive and easily made dessert which will keep for several days in the fridge— the first time I made this someone said 'how very 1970's', which I took as a compliment!

4 conference pears   NOTES
½ bottle cheap red wine
150g castor sugar
thinly pared lemon rind
½ a cinnamon stick
crème fraîche

In a suitably sized pan dissolve the sugar in the red wine, over a low heat, and add the cinnamon , 3 strips of thinly pared lemon rind and ¼ pint water. Simmer for a few minutes.

Meanwhile peel and core the pears, leaving them whole and with the stalks on.

Put the pears, on their sides, in the pan and add more wine or water until they are not quite covered. Cover the pan and simmer gently for 10-15 minutes until the pears are just tender. The time taken will depend on their ripeness.

Remove the pears to a serving dish. Boil the remaining liquid until well reduced and beginning to thicken. Cool for several minutes, strain, and pour over the pears.

Chill for several hours and serve with a swirl of *crème fraîche*.

TIPS AND VARIATIONS-

- you can use cornflour to thicken the sauce but I think reducing gives a more intense flavour
- slice a little off the bottom of the pears and serve them standing upright looks good
- halve the pears to make them go further

RHUBARB AND GINGER
SPONGE PUDDINGS

*For the few weeks when rhubarb is in season these individual
puddings are a delicious combination of tastes*

500g rhubarb

jar of stem ginger in syrup

150g caster sugar

100g unsalted butter

2 eggs

1tsp vanilla essence

125g self raising flour

crème fraîche

6 individual pudding pots

NOTES

Grease the pudding pots and place a small disc of baking paper in the bottom of each; then put 1tbs of the ginger syrup into each pot.

Soften the butter. Coarsely chop 4-5 pieces of the stem ginger. Cut the rhubarb into 1" lengths.

Put the rhubarb into a pan with 50g of the sugar and 2tbs of ginger syrup. Cover and simmer gently for 10 minutes or until softened. Remove the lid and continue to simmer uncovered for 25-30 minutes when it should be a 'dry *purée*'. Let it cool.

Meanwhile put the softened butter with the remaining 100g sugar into a mixing bowl and whisk together until creamy. Gradually beat in the eggs, vanilla, chopped ginger and the flour. Then fold in half of the rhubarb mixture.

Spoon this sponge mixture into the prepared pots, filling each to about two thirds. Put the pots onto a baking tray and into a medium oven, c. 180°C, for 25-30 minutes until golden and risen to fill the pot.

Turn out the puddings, loosening the edges with a knife, and serve immediately, putting the remaining rhubarb mixture on top with a little *crème fraîche*.

TIPS AND VARIATIONS-

- an electric whisk makes life easier
- serve straight from the oven as otherwise the puddings will collapse
- use more or less ginger to taste
- make your own stem ginger- see page 196

RICE PUDDING

Everyone has their own recipe for this - the real secret is long
and very slow cooking –for up to 3 or 4 hours. Sublime!

50g butter

65g caster sugar

100g arborio (pudding) rice

800ml milk

½ vanilla pod

150ml double cream

pinch of salt

NOTES

Melt the butter in the pan and stir in the sugar over a gentle heat until it goes all sticky, using a wooden spoon. Add the rice and continue to stir for a few minutes.

Still on the heat, gradually pour in the milk and stir around to disperse the lumps which will dissolve as the milk heats up. Add the vanilla pod and crush it with the wooden spoon, then stir in the cream and salt and bring to a gentle boil.

Put the pan into a very slow oven, c.145°C, and cook for about 3 hours when it will have developed a lovely creamy texture and the top will have a beautiful golden skin.

Serve warm, as it comes, straight from the oven, or cold if you prefer – but not hot.

TIPS AND VARIATIONS-

- use a heavy wide and shallow metal pan, so that you can start cooking on the hob and then transfer to the oven
- if you haven't a vanilla pod, use ½tsp vanilla essence or try grated nutmeg
- once in the oven do not be tempted to stir again, just let the skin form naturally

TWO SORBETS

Fruit sorbets are quick, easy and fun to make, especially if you have an ice cream maker,
will keep for ages in the freezer and are a useful standby pudding or a palate cleanser

LEMON SORBET

4 lemons
125g granulated sugar
125ml water

NOTES

Cut the lemons into slices, removing pips. Simmer, skin and all, in a covered pan with 1tbs sugar and 2tbs water for 15 minutes until reduced to a *purée*. Liquidise and push through a sieve.

Meanwhile simmer the remaining sugar and water gently for 5 minutes stirring until syrupy.

Let both cool, then stir the syrup into the strained *purée* and put into a plastic freezer container. Put in the freezer and stir every half hour or so until it has completely firmed.

Serve by spooning out appropriately sized portions.

BLACKBERRY SORBET

500g blackberries
2 egg whites
125g granulated sugar
125ml water

NOTES

Make a *purée* of the blackberries, and a syrup, both exactly as for the lemon sorbet. Let them both cool then stir the syrup into the *purée*.

Beat the egg whites until they form 'stiff peaks'. Then fold into the fruit mixture. Put into a plastic container and freeze until ready to use.

Tips and Variations-

* the beaten egg whites give a softer texture and prevent the *purée* from freezing into a solid block. Stirring periodically whilst freezing has the same effect. An ice cream maker will achieve this with less effort
* many different fruits can be used, apple, peach, orange, most soft fruits etc
* generally the citrus fruits, without the egg whites, make a better 'palate cleanser', and the other fruits with egg whites a better dessert

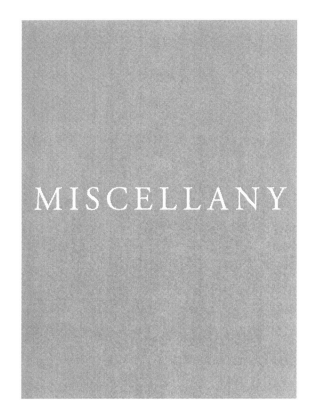

MISCELLANY

THIS BOOK IS intended as my own personal collection of favourite recipes which I have enjoyed cooking, but there are a few odds and ends which do not really fit in to the chapters elsewhere. So here they are.

I love making pickles and chutneys, so satisfying to be able to preserve and make such good use of surplus garden produce in ways other than by freezing. Constant experimentation is called for – in fact once one has understood the basic principles it is really quite difficult to go wrong – and they will always taste better than their commercial equivalents.

Very few people I know have thought of cooking a puffball, indeed most think the idea either horrible, poisonous or both – but they are wrong – it is divine.

Oven baked tomatoes and cheat's Pimms are again both serious ways of proving that cheaper can, so easily and so often, be better.

APPLE AND CUCUMBER CHUTNEY

Another excellent way to make good use of surplus autumn produce

2 large cucumbers

4 -5 large cooking apples

4-5 medium onions

500ml malt vinegar

500g demerara sugar

1tsp salt

2" knob fresh ginger

1tsp each of mustard seeds, allspice and cloves

1½ tsp turmeric

a small to medium red chilli

NOTES

Quarter the cucumbers lengthwise, deseed and coarsely chop. Peel and core the apples and roughly chop. Finely chop the onions. Peel, bruise and finely chop the ginger. Grind together the mustard, allspice and cloves. Deseed the chilli and slice very finely.

Put the apples, cucumber and onion into a large pan with the vinegar. Bring to the boil and simmer gently, uncovered, until softened, about 45-60 minutes.

Add the sugar and stir for a few minutes to dissolve. Then add the salt, ground spices, ginger, chilli and turmeric and continue to simmer, still uncovered, and stirring from time to time, for another 60 minutes or so until the chutney thickens.

Pot into warm jars with sealed lids. Label.

Tips and Variations-

- if using ridge cucumbers peel off the skin which can be rather coarse
- to what degree you chop things is a matter of preference, ie whether you want a chunky or a smoother chutney
- beware that your kitchen will reek of vinegar whilst this is cooking
- you need about 2lbs each of apples and cucumber

A VERY SIMPLE PICKLE

This very easily made uncooked pickle will keep for months
and goes particularly well with spicy Indian dishes

500g sultanas
500g dates
500g cooking apples
500g onions
500ml wine or cider vinegar
300g brown sugar
50g pickling spices in a muslin bag

NOTES

You need a mincing machine for this recipe.

Peel and core the apples. Roughly chop them and the sultanas, the dates, removing stones, and the onions. Put them all through the mincer.

Mix all the fruit together with the vinegar and brown sugar and put in the bag of spices. Leave to stand for 24 hours stirring from time to time. Remove the spice bag and bottle.

CUCUMBER RELISH

Another easily made accompaniment to many Indian dishes

half a cucumber
1dsp salt
1tsp caster sugar
2tbs white wine vinegar
chopped dill, mint or basil

NOTES

Slice the cucumber, skin and all, as thinly as possible. Spread it out and sprinkle over the salt. Leave for 20-30 minutes. Rinse to remove salt. Then drain and squeeze in a clean cloth until dry.

Dissolve the sugar in the vinegar. Stir in the cucumber and the dill.

Chill until ready to use.

CHEAT'S PIMMS

Not many people know this, but one can make a delicious 'home made' Pimms,
for a fraction of the cost of the real thing and arguably rather tastier

1 cup gin

1 cup red vermouth

½ cup orange Curaçao

fizzy lemonade

ice cubes

For The Decoration –

mint leaves

cucumber slices

red currants

strawberry halves

thin slices orange and lemon

Chill all the liquids. In a large jug mix together gin, vermouth and Curaçao. Add your preferred quantity of lemonade and ice cubes.

Add a little of each of the decorating ingredients to your serving glasses and put any remaining in the jug. Serve, ideally in ½ pint glasses, with an ice cube in each.

Tips and Variations-

- normally one would add about 4-5 times the amount of lemonade to alcohol, but vary more or less as to preferred strength
- remember that this a great deal stronger than the 'real' thing
- you don't need all the decorative bits but it's nice to have a colour contrast
- orange Curaçao is not always easily available, so when you see it buy several bottles! and make sure it is the proper thing – there are some 'sherry' strength ones on the market!

FALAFEL

These spicy little chick pea fritters are a very standard
middle eastern snack and equally good hot or cold

250g chick peas   NOTES

large onion

2-3 garlic cloves

1-2tsps ground cumin

1-2tsps ground coriander

pinch of cayenne or chilli powder

handful parsley

salt and pepper

wholemeal flour

sunflower oil

Soak the chick peas in water for several hours or overnight. Then drain, just cover with lightly salted cold water and simmer gently until tender; 1-2 hours. Drain and blend to a thick *purée*.

Meanwhile peel and grate the onion, crush and chop the garlic cloves, chop the parsley and grind the cumin and coriander.

Mix everything together, with the seasoning to taste. Take tablespoonfuls of the mixture and form by hand into small flat patties. Coat with flour and shallow fry in hot oil until brown on both sides.

If the mixture is too dry add a little of the liquor from the cooked chick peas; if too soft put in the fridge for half an hour which will firm it up.

Delicious hot or cold. Serve perhaps with yoghurt or tzatziki.

TIPS AND VARIATIONS-
- soak and cook extra chick peas to make other dishes, such as hoummus
- using tinned chick peas saves a lot of time
- I am told split peas are a good alternative to chick peas
- always better to grind your own spices
- use as a vegetarian burger

FORCE-MEAT BALLS

These are a very tasty accompaniment to many meat or casserole dishes

medium onion

3 bacon rashers

butter

2 slices dry bread

2tbs suet

handful of fresh herbs

1 egg

seasoning

Finely chop the onion. Coarsely chop the bacon and herbs. Process the bread into crumbs. Beat the egg.

Sauté the onion and bacon in a little butter until soft. Add the remaining ingredients and mix well together, binding with the beaten egg.

By hand form into flattish patties – one per person. Fry gently in butter for a few minutes each side until lightly golden.

TIPS AND VARIATIONS-

- try adding some anchovies
- an essential accompaniment to jugged hare –see page 122

GARAM MASALA

A very useful spice mixture to add to many recipes which can be quickly and easily made and is very much better than any ready made versions

1tbs green cardamom seeds

NOTES

half a cinnamon stick

half a nutmeg

1tsp cloves

1tsp black peppercorns

1tsp cumin seeds

Put all the ingredients into a spice grinder, or electric coffee grinder, and grind for 30-40 seconds until all the spices are finely ground.

This make about 4tbs of garam masala. It will keep well and fresh for several weeks if stored in an airtight jar and can be used as and when needed.

Many Indian recipes call for this mixture of spices which is usually added near to the end of the cooking time, or can be sprinkled over a finished dish for a final aromatic flavouring.

TIPS AND VARIATIONS-

- garam masala means hot spice mixture
- every region of India and Pakistan will have its own recipe, as will individual families, but they are all broadly similar to this
- gently dry roast the spices before grinding for a subtly different taste

THE GIANT PUFFBALL

If you are fortunate enough to come across one of these out in the fields in late summer or early autumn, grab it while you can and invite a dozen good friends round immediately for one of life's most utterly delicious, yet simple, gastronomic experiences But don't tell them where you found it!

1 lycoperdon giganteum (giant puffball)

lots of butter

seasoning

NOTES

Puffballs have an intensely rich, penetrating and earthy flavour and can vary enormously in size. They grow very quickly and must be eaten when young and firm and before they degenerate into a mass of tiny spores. At the right time of year you may find them almost anywhere in the open countryside.

Peel away the leathery outer skin and cut the puffball into ½" slices.

Melt butter in a wide pan over a gentle heat and cook the slices, rather like fried bread, until golden brown on each side. They will absorb a lot of butter!

Serve on its own, perhaps with a little seasoning, as a mouth watering *hors d'oeuvre*.

Tips and Variations-
- substitute for mushrooms in a 'greasy spoon' breakfast
- fry them chopped like croutons
- put on top of a steak dish
- flour, egg and breadcrumb the slices, then fry both sides – like a 'schnitzel'
- preserve the puffball by 'drying'. Cut into chunks and let it dry out in the airing cupboard or over the Aga. Store in airtight jars for 6-8 months. Fry or put in casseroles, etc
- thanks to my good friend John for this one

MANGO CHUTNEY

So often with bought mango chutney the bits are all mushed up;
by making your own you can have the mango pieces any size you want!

4-5 large unripe mangoes   NOTES

1tbs salt

500ml white wine vinegar

250g sugar

5 fat garlic cloves

large piece of root ginger

½ tsp cayenne pepper

cinnamon stick

200g raisins or sultanas

Peel the mangoes and cut into slices, removing the stone. Put into a large mixing bowl, cover with water and sprinkle over the salt. Cover and leave for 12 hours or overnight.

Crush and chop the garlic cloves. Peel and finely chop the ginger. Drain and rinse the mangoes.

Put the sugar and vinegar into a large pan and bring slowly to the boil, stirring to dissolve the sugar. Add the mangoes and all the other ingredients and bring back to the boil, continuing to stir. Reduce the heat and simmer, uncovered, stirring from time to time.

After about 30-40 minutes the mixture should be thick and syrupy and the mangoes soft. Remove from the heat, take out the cinnamon stick, and pot.

Tips and Variations-
- it may take more or less time depending on how green are the mangoes
- you can add chopped onions or apple slices if you wish
- you could use less garlic and add some ground roast spices
- if the mangoes are very unripe cover the pan for the first 10 minutes or so

MUSHY PEA FRITTERS

Classically British and all the better for it — not to be confused with avocado mousse!
a traditional accompaniment to fish and chips

250g dried whole green peas

2 small eggs

1tbs melted butter

150g plain flour

150ml milk

seasoning

NOTES

Soak the peas in cold water for several hours or overnight. Drain and rinse them and then simmer in fresh water until soft, about 40-60 minutes.

Drain and briefly process them so that you have a coarse mush. Add the remaining ingredients and mix to a thick *purée.* Season to taste.

Heat a little sunflower oil in a shallow pan. Fry tablespoonfuls of the mixture for a few minutes each side, turning them when a golden brown.

Drain the fritters on kitchen paper and keep warm until ready to serve.

TIPS AND VARIATIONS-

- split peas are okay but not so good
- using a tin of mushy peas saves time!
- for a lighter fritter, separate the eggs and stir in the yolk first, then whisk up the whites until frothy and fold in
- add a little chopped mint
- this recipe is here for my friend Jonathan

OVEN DRIED TOMATOES

*If ever you have a surplus of tomatoes this is a very good and easy way to preserve them.
Not quite such an intense flavour as sun dried tomatoes but sweeter*

8-10 tomatoes

salt

extra virgin olive oil

NOTES

Cut the tomatoes in half horizontally. Scrape out the pips and pulp with a teaspoon. Lightly sprinkle the insides with salt and leave for a few minutes.

Lay the tomatoes, cut side down, on a wire rack with a little space between each which helps the air to circulate.

Put the rack in a very slow oven, approx. 80°C, and leave for 6 to 8 hours. Have a look after 5-6 hours and take out any which seem ready; if you like, turn them over.

When ready they should be chewy with a concentrated sweet tomato flavour.

Pack them into a kilner jar, cover with olive oil and keep until ready to use.

TIPS AND VARIATIONS-

- use medium to larger tomatoes which are ripe but firm
- plum, beef or marmande tomatoes are best as they have more flesh
- leave the oven door very slightly open; the tomatoes should be dried rather than cooked
- preserved in this way they will keep at least one month or longer
- you could put them in an airing cupboard but they would take longer
- use them just as you would sun dried tomatoes
- dry cook them cut side up and sprinkled with crushed garlic, pepper and chopped oregano or basil and a little oil

SOME NIBBLES

A few simple ideas for easily made pre meal tasters- not just crisps and nuts or for a drinks party snacks or a bridge party starter

JELLY'S CHEESY BISCUITS – in a bowl mix together 100g plain flour, 50g mature cheddar cheese, 75g softened butter, ½ tsp baking powder, ¼ tsp cayenne pepper and seasoning. Mix by hand until you have a firm dough (use a food processor if you prefer). Form into a cylinder about 1½" diameter and slice into thin circles. Bake in a medium oven for 20 minutes or so until lightly browned.

SPICED NUTS – bake together a mixture of unsalted nuts; cashew, brazil, peanuts, pecan etc, with olive oil, soy sauce, curry and chilli powders for 15 minutes or so in a medium oven.

HOUMMUS BISCUITS – put a teaspoonful of hoummus onto a small water biscuit and top with a piece of pepperdew or jalapeño pepper, or half a black olive.

MOZZARELLA BALLS - spear baby mozzarella balls with a cocktail stick and add a basil leaf and a sliver of sun (or oven) dried tomato.

PRAWN BLINIS – blini is a traditional Russian pancake and can be easily made, but baby ones are even more easily bought in our supermarkets. Top with *crème fraîche* and half a king prawn with a little black pepper.

DIPS – very 1970's but still just as tasty; little sticks of carrot, celery, cucumber or biscuit dipped in hoummus, guacamole, aubergine *purée,* herring roe or mushroom *pâté,* are all excellent.

CELERY FARCI – cut celery sticks into 1" lengths and fill with stilton.

TIPS AND VARIATIONS-

- if you do smoked salmon on brown bread do at least give a generous salmon portion
- necessity is the mother of invention – you will always find something in your store cupboard to improvise upon
- supermarkets provide an excellent range of very good nibbles, so why bother?
- as everyone has their own ideas I don't really know why I did this page, but Jelly's cheesy biscuits are exceptional and I am quite pleased with the hoummus biscuits

SPICED PEACHES

Most pickles, spiced fruits and chutneys are simply a good means to preserve fruit when there is a glut -but this is well worth making in its own right- quite delicious with cold smoked ham

1½ kg peaches

450ml white wine vinegar

850g granulated sugar

2 cinnamon sticks

1tsp whole allspice

1tsp cloves

you will need several sealable screw top
storage jars

NOTES

If the peaches are ripe enough remove the skins, if not leave them on. Cut into quarters or smaller slices depending on their size.

Tie the cinnamon, allspice and cloves together in a small muslin or cloth bag.

Put the bag of spices into the vinegar in a large pan and bring to the boil. Add the sugar, stir to dissolve and let it simmer, covered, for 10 minutes or so.

Put the sliced peaches into the pan and let them simmer, uncovered, until just tender. This will take from 5-30 minutes depending on their size and ripeness.

Remove the peaches with a slotted spoon and pack into the warm clean jars. Boil the vinegar to reduce a little – it should be nicely syrupy. Strain into the jars, covering the peaches, and screw down the lids.

They should keep well for a year or more but wait at least 4 weeks before using.

TIPS AND VARIATIONS-

- this recipe is probably best with fruit that is slightly unripe
- you can substitute cider vinegar for wine vinegar
- it doesn't really matter if you leave the skins on
- this recipe works well with plums or nectarines

STEM GINGER IN SYRUP

This is easy and fun to make and although probably not quite so good as its commercial equivalent it is nonetheless well worthwhile having a go

medium size root of ginger

500ml water

250g granulated sugar

NOTES

Peel the ginger and cut into julienne strips, or little cubes if you prefer.

Bring a large pan of water to the boil and blanch the ginger for 10-15 seconds. Drain and repeat the process two more times using fresh water in each case.

Put the 500ml water in medium sized pan, bring to the boil and dissolve the sugar. Add the drained ginger and simmer gently for 20-30 minutes. Allow to cool.

Remove the ginger pieces and put in an screwtop jar, pouring in enough syrup to cover. Store until ready to use.

TIPS AND VARIATIONS-

- the younger the ginger the better; older and more fibrous ginger needs more blanching
- this will keep for a long time, ideally in the fridge

PRESERVED GINGER – dry your pieces of stem ginger, use the syrup in a pudding; roll in granulated sugar and store in an airtight jar. Delicious little nibbles.

GROUND GINGER – cut peeled root ginger into very small pieces and dry for 24 hours in a very low oven, or airing cupboard. When completely dried put into a spice grinder and whiz until you have a fine powder. Store in an airtight jar.

TOMATO AND BROAD BEAN BRUSCHETTA

An easily made and very delicious snack

350g broad beans
2 firm but ripe avocado pears
2-3 large ripe tomatoes
4 thick slices of soda bread
6-8 very thin slices Parma ham
2 fat garlic cloves
250g mozzarella cheese
2 lemons
3-4tbs olive oil

NOTES

Boil the beans for 3-4 minutes until just cooked. Cool and then remove the skins.

Halve the avocados. Remove the skin and stone. Cut into thick slices.

Skin the tomatoes, deseed and coarsely chop.

Mix all the above together in a large bowl together with the juice of one of the lemons.

Toast the bread and when cool rub one side with the peeled garlic cloves.

Roll up the ham in a bundle and slice into ribbons. Cut the mozzarella into smallish pieces. Make a dressing with oil and juice of the remaining lemon.

Put a piece of toast, garlic side up, onto each serving plate. Pile the salad on top and scatter over the ham ribbons and cheese. Drizzle over the dressing and a little seasoning.

TIPS AND VARIATIONS-

- bruschetta is basically toast, rubbed with garlic and topped with olive oil
- one can think of an imaginative variety of toppings for experimentation
- any coarse country bread, and any good smoked ham will do
- skinning broad beans is very tedious, but by golly its worth it
- make your own soda bread – see page 62

TWO GOOD STUFFINGS FOR A TURKEY

Everyone has their own best way to cook a turkey, but these two stuffings –
one for each end of the bird – are favourites and are very easy to make.

A PRUNE AND CHESTNUT STUFFING-

15-20 large stoned prunes   NOTES

¼ bottle red wine

large head of celery

2 medium onions

butter

1 tbs dried mixed herbs

2 lemons

1 lb prepared chestnuts

seasoning

Simmer the prunes in the wine, uncovered, for 15- 20 minutes. Remove the prunes and boil the liquid until well reduced and reserve.

Coarsely chop the celery and the onion. Grate the rind from the lemons and roughly break the chestnuts into pieces.

In a large pan or wok melt some butter and simmer the onion and celery until softening, 15-20 minutes. Remove from the heat.

Add the prunes, lemon rind, herbs and chestnuts. Stir lightly, season well and add the reduced wine. When cooled enough gently stuff the back end of your bird.

A SIMPLE SAUSAGE STUFFING -

700g spicy sausage meat   NOTES

2 thick slices bread

medium onion

250g mushrooms

seasoning and an egg

4 rashers streaky bacon

Crumb the bread in a liquidiser, finely chop the onion, the mushrooms and the bacon.

Mix everything well together and carefully stuff the front end of your bird.

TIPS AND VARIATIONS-

- these should be about enough for a good 12-15lb turkey
- use fresh herbs if available
- if you have any stuffing left over, fry as stuffing balls

INDEX

all recipe titles appear in bold

Lightning Source UK Ltd.
Milton Keynes UK
UKOW010840140812

197491UK00001B/18/P